# DEAR BULLY

## 70 AUTHORS TELL THEIR STORIES

# DEAR BULLY

## 70 AUTHORS TELL THEIR STORIES

*edited by*

## MEGAN KELLEY HALL *&* CARRIE JONES

HARPER TEEN

*An Imprint of HarperCollinsPublishers*

HarperTeen is an imprint of HarperCollins Publishers.

See pages 367–369 for complete copyright listing.

Dear Bully: Seventy Authors Tell Their Stories
www.epicreads.com

Library of Congress Cataloging-in-Publication Data
Dear bully : seventy authors tell their stories / edited by Carrie Jones and
Megan Kelley Hall. — 1st ed.
    p.    cm.
    ISBN 978-0-06-206098-3 (tr. bdg.)
    ISBN 978-0-06-206097-6 (pbk. bdg.)
    1. Bullying—United    States—Juvenile    literature.    2.    School
discipline—United States.    I. Jones, Carrie.    II. Kelley Hall, Megan.
BF637.B85D43   2011                                  2011010166
302.3—dc22                                                  CIP
                                                             AC

Typography by Andrea Vandergrift
11  12  13  14  15   LP/RRDB   10 9 8 7 6 5 4 3 2 1
❖
First Edition

*For our daughters*

# Contents

# Introduction

# Why Do We Celebrate Bullying?
## BY ELLEN HOPKINS

I know bullying. Personally and through my children. In elementary school, I was smart. Sort of pretty. A talented equestrian, singer, dancer, and creative writer. I was also chubby. Not obese. Not even fat, really. But not a skinny jeans kind of girl. You know, the kid who other kids called "Elsie the cow." Luckily, I was strong—the kid who let insults roll off her because she knew in her heart she was destined to do great things.

That strength came from my parents, who believed in me. In turn, I believe in my children. My oldest son, Jason, is gay. He knew it before I did, and so when the bullying began, he knew why. But I didn't. Never underestimate the power of a mother bear, and I became one. At the time, bullying wasn't new, but confronting it was. School counselors told

1

me to leave it alone. Things would get better. They didn't. To escape the torment in California, Jason chose to live with his father (my ex) in New Mexico.

My youngest child, Orion, is almost fourteen. He isn't gay, but he is chubby. He was teased some in elementary school, but the real bullying began last year, in seventh grade. One kid was largely at the heart of it. I started hearing his name in September, when he began calling Orion gay. Why does that term, accurate or not, jumpstart abusive behavior? Over the course of the year, this kid and his friends volleyed relentless verbal attacks that eventually became physical. Orion was shoved, pushed to the ground, hit, and once had his head slammed into a locker.

This time the school had no choice but to get involved. Suspending the bully for a day or five didn't really faze him, however. I tried calling his parents. His mother's reaction was, "My child would never do such a thing." But he did, and it continued until one afternoon when Orion was followed off the school bus by a friend of the bully's—a high school senior—who grabbed Orion by the throat with both hands. Fortunately, a passerby prevented what might have been an even worse incident. I'd had enough. I called the sheriff, who sent a deputy to address the issue. The bully's parents brought him over to apologize. This year, everything seems to be in a holding pattern.

Orion is not alone. The statistics, in fact, are staggering. From 2009 surveys we find:

- More than seventy-five percent of our students are subjected to harassment by a bully or cyberbully and experience physical, psychological, and/or emotional abuse.

- More than twenty percent of our kids admit to being a bully or participating in bullylike activities.

- On a daily average 160,000 children miss school because they fear they will be bullied if they attend classes.

- On a monthly average 282,000 students are physically attacked by a bully.

Surprised? Why? Not only do many Americans tolerate bullying, they stand in the wings and cheer it on. In fact, there lately seems to be a real celebration of violent attacks against people who are different. If you don't believe me, spend a little time reading the comments following a news story about, oh, say, a mosque burning on U.S. soil.

Forget the fact that most of these people are citizens of the United States of America—a country founded on the principles of religious freedom. Yet because Muslims are "different," they are bullied, in much the same way a child who is different is bullied at school. Chubby or skinny; geek smart or challenged; gay or perceived that way;

black, brown, yellow, or any color other than the person hurling insults. Any of these things can make someone a target.

Some might argue this is simply the evolutionary byproduct of survival of the fittest. That all animals weed out the weak. But the human animal has a brain capable of compassion. What's lacking is the will to embrace someone who's different. Not only are we reminded daily of those differences by loud-mouthed pundits, but those same political shock jocks encourage fear-based reactions to those who are different. They whip their listeners into frenzied overreactions, with results like the cab driver who was shot for admitting his religious affiliation. Or places of worship being torched.

Picking on others is learned behavior. The kid who manifests violence has learned violence somewhere. Too often, that somewhere is home. Parents should teach their children to respect diversity. But if they won't, others must step in. It *does* take a village to raise a child who embraces all people, regardless of their differences. Which means we must take action whenever we suspect bullying. Does that make you uncomfortable? Consider these statistics:

- Every seven minutes a child is bullied on a school playground, with more than eighty-five percent of those instances occurring without any intervention.

- Surveys from 2009 show that more than 100,000 children carry guns to school as a result of being bullied.

- Twenty-eight percent of students who carry weapons in school have witnessed violence in their homes.

- Forty-six percent of males and twenty-six percent of females admit to having been involved in physical fights as a result of being bullied.

- More than eighty-five percent of our teenagers say that revenge as an aftermath of being bullied is the leading cause for school shootings and homicide.

- A child commits suicide as a direct result of being bullied once every half hour, with 19,000 bullied children attempting to commit suicide over the course of one year.

Despite those sobering stats, more than half of all bullying events are never reported at all. So it is our job, as that village, to stand up and take notice. To care enough about every child—mainstream or somehow different—to ensure his or her safety. That means speaking out boldly against any acts of violence toward those who are different. And also teaching our children that our unique traits make us special, not something to be feared, taunted, or pushed toward suicide.

The authors whose stories follow have chosen to speak out boldly, to unite in a call to action against bullying. They have been bullied. And they have bullied. Hindsight brings a broad perspective to these acts. By sharing their wider view, they hope you'll choose to join our village. To help us create safe communities, homes, and schools, where everyone is valued for who they are, not in spite of their differences but because of them.

# DEAR BULLY

# Dear Bully

## BY LAURIE FARIA STOLARZ

Dear Bully,

I'm not sure if you remember me. But I definitely remember you. You were my first real bully—the boy who made me fear getting out of bed in the morning, who made me dread the end of the weekend because I'd have to see you the next day, and who prompted me to take self-defense classes.

I never knew that boys could be so cruel.

Until I met you.

It was middle school—seventh grade for me, eighth grade for you—and we took the school bus together every morning and afternoon. We didn't know each other. To this day, we've never had a full conversation. We didn't hang out in any of the same circles, nor were we members of any opposing clubs or teams.

So you had no reason to hate me.

9

But still you did. Or at least you treated me as though you did.

I remember the first time I saw you: slick dark hair, designer jeans, high-top sneakers, and a leather jacket. That one outfit probably cost more than my entire wardrobe at the time. Was it my lack of style that made me a target? Or the fact that I didn't fight back too hard?

At first it was just name-calling: *dumbdorkstupiduglytrash bagbitchlosercuntuglyassholestuckupsnottyassbitchnastyidiot snobmoronstupidasswipedildoloserscumbaguglybitchdouchebag.* I'd stare out the window of the bus, trying not to show any hint of emotion, even though I could feel it all over my face. I knew that others were looking, too, checking for my reaction. I'd bite the inside of my cheek just shy of drawing blood, pretending that I was someplace else, wishing that you'd get bored when I didn't respond. But instead you just got more people involved. Other boys (not all, but some) were drawn to you and helped you out with your ridicule. I'd be called a stuck-up snob when I ignored all of you, and then a nasty-ass bitch when I didn't.

If any of my friends were around, they kept a distance from me for their own survival. Eventually they stopped taking the bus altogether, opting to have a parent drive them instead. Sometimes I was able to hitch a ride. But more often than not, I'd end up back at the bus stop.

Back with you.

It went on for months like this before things got physical.

Before you started pushing me from behind, shoving me out into the street at the bus stop, tugging my hair, pulling at my clothes, slapping the back of my head, and spitting in my face. While your cohorts thought it was funny as hell, others stayed out of it, most likely relieved that it was me you were harassing and not them.

The route home was the worst because our bus didn't show up until thirty minutes after we were let out for the day.

Thirty minutes.

Without a single teacher or administrator to monitor what was going on.

Thirty minutes.

For you to try to keep yourself occupied. That's where I came in.

People told me that if I ignored you, if I pretended that you didn't bother me, you'd eventually give up and move on to the next victim.

So why didn't that ever happen?

It was hard for my mom to hear about the terrible time I was having with you. She was working a full- and a part-time job and couldn't be there to bring me to school or pick me up. She begged the principal to have a teacher stick around at the end of the school day until the bus came. The principal agreed.

But it never happened.

My mother told the principal that you were the one harassing me and that it was his job to ensure a safe environment for children. Again, he agreed.

But again, he did nothing.

And so one morning, one of my older brothers, the captain of the high school football team at the time, decided to accompany me to the bus stop. He got into your face. Threatened you. And pushed you back a couple times.

In that moment, you seemed intimidated. Your cohorts certainly were. But while they stopped harassing me completely (and even apologized for it), you continued the very next day.

One afternoon, the following week, it was raining and the bus didn't come until an hour after school got out for the day. And in that time, you managed to push me down onto the pavement and kick me with mud, until I was covered. Until it was in my hair, and in my ears, and up inside the crevices of my mouth.

I remember getting up, tears streaming down my cheeks, and seeing you laughing.

And wondering how anyone could be so mean.

That was the last time I took the bus. From then on I walked to and from school. It took me just shy of an hour and would've been well worth two.

I didn't see you much after that. Then I heard you'd moved away. A couple years later, I changed schools.

And then flash forward about fifteen years: I was in my twenties, working in the writing center of a college. My job was to assist students with their essays and research papers.

One night, just before my shift was over, a student came in, wanting me to help her with an interview assignment. She was asked to interview someone whom she really looked up to and respected, and then to write an essay based on her findings.

To my complete and utter shock that someone was you.

The interview detailed your whole life's story, from early childhood—a story that had been anything but charmed (to say the least)—and how, despite all odds, you'd been able to turn things around for yourself (which is why the student chose you for the assignment).

I won't go into your life's details here—because they're your details to share, not mine—but suffice it to say that in that moment, reading that student's interview about how life had been for you growing up, I couldn't condone any of the things you'd done to me in the past, but I could almost understand why you'd done them.

After the student left the writing center, I couldn't believe what a coincidence it was—that out of all the schools and all the writing tutors, that girl just happened to make an appointment with me.

But then I wondered if maybe it wasn't a coincidence at all—if maybe it was meant to be, that I was meant to see you in a different way and understand you a little better.

And now I think I do.

No longer your victim,
Laurie Faria Stolarz

# Love Letter to My Bully
## BY TONYA HURLEY

Dear Steven,

You never forget your first.

The first time you were forced to eat pink-colored glue on the bus and were told it was gum even though you knew it wasn't. The first time you were snapped in the ear with a rubber band in algebra class and were made to sit still in your seat despite telling the teacher, who was also afraid, all while trying to figure out the value for $x$. The first time you were shaken down for lunch money or tripped in the hallway or the first time you were forced to cower in fear on the school bus or were humiliated in front of teachers and classmates in ways you could have scarcely imagined. The first time, tears streaming down your face, the teacher told you to "stand up for yourself" but did nothing to help. The first time your virginity was publicly disputed in graphic detail before you even really knew what *virginity* meant. The first time your innocence was taken from you, your faith in people and your illusions about the world and your place in it were thoroughly and irretrievably shattered.

I tried to deal with you, Steven, in any number of ways—by ignoring you, avoiding you, reporting you, and eventually even fighting with you. As I've gotten older, I've psychoanalyzed you in hopes of trying to understand you, to figure out how people can be so awful to one another, whether it's learned behavior or genetic predisposition. I've tried to excuse you, putting your callousness down to a bad upbringing, broken home, lack of discipline, insecurity, or maybe just a lack of love in your life and compassion in your soul. I've even tried to forgive you, although I have to admit that hasn't worked out very well. Like some unwelcome ex-boyfriend who friends you on Facebook or an embarrassing prom date who pops up in old family photo albums, you are unavoidable, even all these years later. My daughter even knows your name.

As must be obvious by now, I've spent a lot of time pondering you, some might even say obsessing over you. Way too much, in fact. I've searched for you on the internet to find out who you are now and what you're up to these days, not because I care, but perhaps for an opportunity to gloat. I've dreamed about getting revenge on you more times than

I can count. And if I ran into you on the street today, I would have just two words to say. Thank. You.

Your cruelty and insensitivity were a wake-up call, a lesson in life I would not have learned otherwise at such a young age. You prepared me for the world beyond our small town. More than anything, you motivated me. Because no matter how hard I tried to block you out, some of your insults, your criticism, stuck with me, eating at me, making me doubt myself, until I had no choice but to persevere and to succeed. If for no other reason than to show you. See, without you, there would be no me, at least not the me I came to be.

Every time I struggled with a difficult college course, a hopeless job interview, a terse rejection letter, a thankless boss, a petty colleague, a bad relationship, or just some impatient jerk on the subway, it was your face I saw. You have taken many shapes and forms since, but after all these years, it's still you. Our relationship is a special one, and I've learned that no one can take your place. From you, I realized that life is harsh and not always fair. I learned that not everyone is well-intentioned. I realized that not everyone will like you or respect you, no matter what you do or how much you try to please everyone. I learned to rely on myself, to believe in myself, to do for myself, and to fight for myself. Having family and friends to provide a shoulder to cry on is a wonderful thing, and I've taken advantage of their love and kindness more times than I can count, but it is your adversaries that strengthen you, that toughen you, that sharpen you, that force you to be the best you can be, to keep trying no matter how difficult the task or unachievable the goal, to prove them wrong.

Because you victimized me, I no longer allow myself to be victimized. You broke my bully cherry and I've never been the same.

Love,
Tonya

# Dear Audrey

## BY COURTNEY SHEINMEL

Dear Audrey[*],

I'm counting on the fact that you'll never pick up this book. After twenty years, there's an enormous part of me that feels choked up by the thought of you, afraid to open my mouth because what I say might make it worse. At least when I finish this, the things I bottled up will be there, in writing.

Except now I don't even know how to start.

We were friends in seventh grade; for a few months, we hung out together after school nearly every single day. Then, I remember, you started spending a little bit less time with me and little bit more with Jessica Searle. At lunch,

---

[*] Names and other identifying details have been changed, and certain individuals are composites.

you stopped caring whether I saved the seat next to me. My mother noticed you didn't call so much anymore, and when I told her I thought maybe you wanted to be Jessica's best friend instead, she assured me that you'd come around. Maybe the problem was that I kept inviting you to things; maybe I should have just left you alone. One day you pulled a Bloomingdale's catalog out of your locker. It must have been during study hall, because in my head I see a few of us sprawled out in the hallway, uniform skirts rolled up and boxer shorts worn underneath, our attempt at modesty. You flipped the book open and pointed to different items, a pair of leggings, a sweater with patches on the elbows, and asked whether I liked them.

The phone rang that night and my mother came into my room. "Audrey for you," she said with a smile—a smile that meant, *You see, I told you so.*

When I picked up, you said, "I can't believe you actually liked those overalls—they're so immature. And that pink baby-doll dress was hideous."

There was a muffled sound and I asked you what it was. You pretended that you hadn't heard a thing. Then you said maybe your sister had picked up the extension. But I knew you were calling me on three-way, probably with Jessica Searle, and when I hung up the two of you would stay on the line and talk about how awful I was, how babyish and inferior. I'd done the same thing with you a couple months before. You called Beth Fogel and asked what she was planning to wear to Lorelai Martin's birthday party, even though you knew full well she hadn't been invited.

It occurred to me just how mean we'd been to Beth, and I was sorry for that; but even more, I worried about turning into someone exactly like her.

As time went by, you picked on the things that most embarrassed me and found flaws I didn't even know I had. You laughed at my fear of elevators, at my tendency to refer to my childhood babysitter as a big sister. You told Señora Baldwin that I cheated off your Spanish quiz, just because I dared to sit in the seat next to yours. You said I should meet you at our old pizza place, and then you never showed up. I thought it was my fault: I was too short, I wasn't pretty enough, I didn't like the right music, my parents didn't have enough money. I didn't stand up for myself, ever, and now I wonder if part of the problem was that I never confronted you; instead I retreated and cried in private. But I suspect it was something else entirely, something I won't ever get to know. Something like that indefinable chemistry between two people when they like each other, except the opposite.

Then you started complaining about having little headaches. They came often and you said Tylenol did nothing to relieve them. I thought maybe you had a brain tumor, and I felt guilty for every bad thought I'd ever had about you. We were in eighth grade by then, the summer had done nothing to subdue your distaste for me, and we had a class meeting to vote on our song for the Middle School Sing Off.

Miss Halloran stepped out of the room and you dropped your head down toward the desk, pressing your fingers into your temples. "Oh, my little headache," you moaned. "I just can't get rid of it."

Jessica Searle hit you in the side and you both started laughing. Lorelai Martin turned to me. We hadn't been friends in a long time; she'd always been more your friend than mine, so it made sense that she'd pulled away when you did. But suddenly she had a look of such compassion on her face, and she said, "You know what she's talking about, don't you."

It was more of a statement than a question, and it hit me all at once, like a punch to the gut.

"Little Headache" was your nickname for me. And everyone knew.

My cheeks were burning and there was this feeling coming from deep inside me, as strong as anything I'd ever felt before: I was ashamed to just be myself. In all of my life, I've never felt that again quite so strongly. Even now, I can't even write about it without wanting to cry. Even now, I feel the heat on my cheeks and something flapping inside my chest.

You left school a year later, and by the end of ninth grade, things started to turn around for me. For a long time, I had fantasies of bumping into you on the street, preferably when I was surrounded by friends. Maybe I would become a world-famous writer, and then you'd read about me. Or I could marry a movie star, and you'd see our wedding covered on *Entertainment Tonight.* It's funny that even as I've gotten older, my desire to prove my worth to you has not dimmed that much. The friends I have today are the coolest, most extraordinary group of people I've ever known, and they are loyal, and they are plentiful, and they are mine. It is as if I think that if you saw how good it was now, it would make the reality even more valid.

A few months back I heard about a horrible story out of Florida: A fifteen-year-old girl had been severely beaten. Her attacker was a troubled boy whose brother had committed suicide. The boy had been dating the victim's best friend, and when the victim purportedly said something to her best friend about her boyfriend's dead brother, something inside him snapped. He was arrested and I think tried for attempted murder, though I'm not sure what his sentence was.

Reading about those kids, my stomach turning, I was overwhelmed by their pain. My own story of adolescent cruelty seemed so simple, so harmless. I didn't even ever get slammed into a locker; certainly no one was bringing weapons to school. But of course it doesn't need to end in tragedy to be transformative.

For better or worse, Audrey, you changed my life.

With pride, I remain,
Courtney

# Slammed

## BY MARLENE PEREZ

When I saw the book just lying there on the bleachers, I wondered if you had left it there on purpose. If you had left it for me to see all those hateful things people said about me. About everyone.

No one had passed the slam book my way. What would I have done if they did? I'd like to think that I would have done the right thing and not written anything.

I turned to my page first. Now I understood why they called it a slam book. Because when I read what was written about me, I felt as though an invisible person was repeatedly slamming me into a wall. I couldn't even see who I was fighting.

Or could I? After I shook away the tears, my vision cleared and I recognized almost everyone's handwriting.

A guy from my chemistry class, the one who would smile

at me sometimes, wrote about how I'd performed a certain sexual favor for him. The only place that ever happened was in his imagination. And there was stuff from people who I thought were my friends, too. People like you. I recognized your handwriting right away but couldn't believe you had written those things. That my boobs were too big and that my brain was too small.

We weren't *best* friends or anything, but I thought we were friends. What about all those games we'd ridden to together? We double-dated for homecoming when we were sophomores. Remember? I held your hair back when you threw up all that cheap wine you and your date were guzzling. We talked about how your brother had died and even about getting out of this town, moving somewhere far away where nobody knew us.

I thumbed through the book and saw your handwriting on every page. You hated so many people, but most of all, I think you hated yourself.

I thought I knew you, but I didn't. I thought we were friends, but we weren't. Then you walked back into the gym, a panicked look on your face. You didn't see me right away, so I slid the book into my backpack.

"What's the matter? Lose something?" I asked.

You frowned, the panic on your face growing. "It's not important."

I met your eyes.

"I thought I lost something, too," I said. "Turns out I never even had it."

# My Apology

## BY MARINA COHEN

## 1981

I look up at the wall. It's 3:25. The second hand appears to be moving more quickly than usual, like it's racing around the face of the ugly black clock. Each second brings me closer to the end of the day.

Heads keep turning, stealing glances at me as though they might divine my thoughts. I pretend I don't see. I sit statue still. I hear whispering all around. Can't the teacher hear it? She's busy making sure we're clear on our assignments for the next day. She has no clue. They rarely do.

I reach up and remove my earrings one at a time. They are real gold. My grandmother brought them all the way from Italy. She'd be so disappointed if I lost one. I tuck them safely into the pocket of my jeans.

The whispering is getting louder. The teacher tells the

students to be quiet now, but she has no idea what the buzz is all about. I worry what my face looks like. My cheeks feel hot, burning, but I keep my eyes hard, my expression blank. I can't let them see how scared I am.

The bell silences the din. For a second, I feel everyone's stares tunneling into my skin. Then they stand up. They get their coats and books. Suddenly I'm holding my jean jacket and books, too. I must have picked them up but I don't even register doing so. Everything is a blur of sound and movement as I drift into the hall and out the door. The vultures follow. They circle ravenously. I can hear them talking; their voices spill over with excitement. "Are you going through with it?" "Is it true?" I don't answer them. I can't lose focus. My throat is chalk dry. I try to swallow, but it hurts.

Outside, tornadoes of litter and leaves twist about. I'm jealous of the chocolate bar wrapper that is snatched up and carried away. I want the wind to carry me away, too, away from all of this, but I'm cast-iron heavy. Dead weight.

Then the crowd parts as if perfectly choreographed and I see them. They stand high on the cement steps. They look confident together. I stand in the middle of a crowd and yet I'm all alone. They make no move toward me so I take a step closer to them. My heart feels like it's going to explode. I clench my fists to keep my fingers from trembling.

I walk until I'm face-to-face with her. She refuses to look at me. Her eyes shift between the faces of her friends. She is smiling, chatting, laughing. I stare right at her, forcing my eyes cold, lifeless.

The vultures begin to squawk. They want action. They thirst for it. But this isn't what drives me forward. I just want this to be over. I've had enough. It all ends today.

Finally, she shifts her focus. She looks me in the eye, and for a split second, I see something I've never seen before. It surprises me. So much so that I take a step back. In her sparkling green eyes, her laughing and mocking green eyes, do I see correctly? Do I detect a trace of fear? This amuses me. It almost derails me. I almost turn to leave, but then she speaks.

"Well," she says. "I'm not going to start this."

Sparks of anger ignite my insides. Her words thunder in the air around me. *You don't want to start this?* I want to scream. I want to explode. Tears burn at the backs of my eyes. *You don't want to start this?* All these years, and now you say you don't want to start this?

My mind goes blank. The crowd melts away. I see nothing but her green eyes filled with contempt and fear. My hand rests at my side. My fist unclenches. My arm slices through the crisp air. I make contact.

# 2011

*Dear Kristie,*

*I'm very sorry I slapped you in the yard after school. I wish I could say I didn't mean to, but that would be a lie. We both know it was no accident. I hit you. I admit it. And now I'm apologizing because I know I was wrong.*

*Thing is, I was so tired of you and Brenda and the rest of your gang calling me names. Mostly "Dog." Every single time I passed you in class, in the yard, or in the hall. What kind of a dog did you think I was, anyway? A poodle? A Doberman? Just curious. Particularly hurtful was when you'd just shorten your insults to "ruff, ruff," barking in my direction, looking at one another and laughing. You were relentless. I don't even know what I ever did to you to deserve this treatment. Was it because I wasn't a follower? Was it because I spoke my mind? Were you so threatened by me? Were you so afraid your control over others would diminish if just one person challenged your beliefs? I guess you had to figure out a way to silence me. Demeaning. Discrediting. Excluding. These are all just forms of silencing, aren't they?*

*I have no excuse for my terrible actions that day, but I realize now, I struck you because I simply didn't have the words—the words to express all the pain, the frustration, the feelings of self-doubt, of shame, of embarrassment you caused me. I didn't have the words then—but I have them now, so I say to you and all others like you:*

My self-worth is not linked to your cruel words and actions.

My self-esteem is not affected by your deliberate attempts to destroy my character.

You have no power over me.

You will not silence me.

*These words are not constructed of ink and paper. They are not formed of movement and sound. They are echoes of my soul. May they ripple outward and give strength to those who hear them.*

*Sincerely,*
*Marina*

# Dear Samantha
## BY KIERAN SCOTT

Dear Samantha,

I'm writing you this letter because there's something I've been dying to ask. How did you do it? How did you manage to have so much control over so many of us? Even more intriguing . . . how did you *know* you *could* do it? What gave you the confidence to roll into middle school that first day of fifth grade and take over? Did you sense we were all weaker than you? That we weren't as smart? How did you decide who to pick off first? Who was least worthy of your "friendship"?

Back in fifth, when you made Aura Montrose walk up to me in homeroom and declare loudly that I was clearly anorexic, that I obviously needed help, that I had to stop with my psychotic disease or I was going to kill myself, I was mortified, dumbstruck, destroyed. To this day I remember everyone laughing—Evan Lawrence's openmouthed cackle, Danielle Jennings's sympathetic glance, Jenny Marx standing behind Aura with that awful, triumphant smirk. That was the day you decided that I was no longer worthy, and just like that, I was no longer popular, either. After that day, it was just me and Mary, the one person who stayed by my side, my BFF. For the next few weeks I would sit in the cafeteria and watch you, surrounded by all your (formerly my) friends, and wonder what I did wrong. Was it my pink tube socks? Was it because my brother was being picked on by the "cool" kids in his grade? Was my house not big enough or my backpack too large or my hair too straight? Why did all those girls get to remain in the inner circle while I was kicked out? I felt so uncool. So unlucky. And I didn't know why.

But as time went on, I realized that I was actually one of the lucky ones. Because as you got older, you got crueler. Coercing people into signing that anti–Cara Mellon petition; that awful "gift" you sent to Maya Walters that was supposedly from the guy she liked. Even Aura and Jenny, in the end, weren't immune from your tactics. (Perhaps Jenny's smirk that day was her gloating over the fact that it wasn't *her* day. That she would live to see another as part of your in crowd. But it didn't last long, did it?) You embarrassed and ostracized each and every one of us until my table, the outcast table, was more crowded than yours. Until we were the ones having fun at lunch while you were practically alone. I learned not to blame those who did your bidding, who stood by and smirked, because I knew that if I had been in their position, I would have stood by and said nothing. Let you do your thing. Because standing up to you was just too scary to contemplate. I tried to understand where they were coming from, and I forgave them. In hindsight I realize that if we had all just stood up to you the first time you "pulled a Samantha," most of us never would have had to suffer. I wonder what you would have done if ten girls had all told you to stop. If ten girls had come to you as one and told you what we really, truly thought of you. What I wouldn't give for a big, fat rewind button.

By the time you'd whittled your inner circle down to three, I had seen enough. Enough to know that *you* were no longer worthy of *my* attention, not even my curiosity. I knew that if you ever tried to hurt me again, you would find that you were incapable. That if you ever tried to hurt anyone else, I wouldn't be a part of it. Clearly we didn't need you or your approval. We were just fine being us.

So I guess I'm really writing this letter to say thank you. I believe that it was because of the way you treated me that I learned what really mattered. It was because of the way you treated me that I learned to be my own person, have my own opinion, stand my ground. It's at least partially because I survived you that I'm the person I am today.

And I like me.

~~Love,~~

~~xoxo~~

Sincerely,

Kieran Scott

JUST KIDDING

# Stench

## BY JON SCIESZKA

His real name was Michael Henry. Which should have been funny enough . . . considering the average level of our fifth-grade wit.

For instance:

Because he was short, we called Bobby D. "Shorty."

Because he had white-blond hair, we called Timmy G. "Whitey."

And it won't take you much brainpower to guess what we called Mike W., who happened to have the biggest, most stuck-out ears in the entire school.

Yes, "Ears."

So we really should have called Michael Henry something like "Two First Names" or "Mike Hank." But I guess we didn't have a nickname for Michael Henry because he was new to school.

He was a big kid. Chubby and dark brown. He even had a hint of black mustache hairs on his upper lip. There were rumors that he had been held back a grade. Or maybe two. And because Michael Henry was older than us, he was also further into adolescence than us, and hadn't had that deodorant talk with his mom. He smelled.

I, on the other hand, with a September birthday, was one of the youngest and smallest kids in fifth grade. I had avoided getting tagged with an embarrassing nickname mostly by keeping a low profile—cracking the occasional joke, not messing with the bigger guys, and generally not drawing any attention to myself.

So it was kind of unusual that I even said anything in the group of fifth-grade boys hanging around the playground after lunch that day. But I did.

Bill M., the captain of our fifth-grade basketball team, was trying out nicknames for Michael Henry, who was standing right there with us. "How about 'Round Guy'?"

"Bigfoot," suggested Whitey.

"Big Head!" said Shorty.

"Really Dark Hair Guy!" said Ears.

The fifth-grade boy brain has a terrifying power. In the presence of other fifth-grade boy brains, it is capable of joining together with those brains . . . and somehow generating less thoughtful action than any one of the individual brains. Which is exactly what happened next.

I don't know why I violated my own survival strategy of laying low. I must have been still drunk on a feeling of word power from my 100 percent on the third-period vocabulary test. I joined in the fifth-grade brain drain and blurted out a single word—"Stench!"

Everybody looked at me.

"It means a really bad smell," I added.

"Stench," repeated Bill M., trying it out. "Hey, Stench," Bill M. said to Michael Henry. And that was that. Michael Henry was Stench for the rest of fifth grade.

I honestly didn't give it much more thought. If anything, I was pretty pleased that Bill M. had taken my suggestion and that everybody now knew I was a pretty smart word guy. Another terrifying power of the fifth-grade boy brain: the ability to not even think about how your actions might affect others. I had no idea how much misery that one small mean word caused Michael Henry.

But in a fitting turn of the karmic wheel, the next year, in sixth grade, my mom bought me a pair of green corduroy pants. These pants were a shade of green just bright enough to catch the attention of Bill M. He took one look at them and called to me, "Hey. Nice pants, Green Bean."

And so I was "Green Bean" for the whole first half of sixth grade. No matter what pants I wore.

Sorry about the "Stench" nickname, Michael H.

I hope "Green Bean" evened things up a bit.

And here's hoping that maybe this story will help a fifth grader out there fight against the mind-sucking power of the no-think group brain.

# What I Wanted to Tell You
## BY MELISSA SCHORR

E—

*Can you even believe it? We made it? Junior high is actually over???*

I can. I've only been praying for the last 231 nights or so for someone to come and put an end to my misery. All I can say is: What took so long?

*There are soooo many memories I have of the two of us. Remember playing pranks on my patio? Doing backflips at your pool? Sex ed with Mr. Mueller? Good times . . .*

Until the moment you decided I wasn't cool enough or fun enough or whatever enough to be your friend anymore. And dropped me, like a stone down a cold, dark shaft.

*This year was a total blast, you know?*

Well, that's how it looked, anyway, from my perch in social Siberia. Because with you waltzed every last one of my so-called friends. Karen and Shoshana. Gia and Gaby. Sarah and Sabrina. Pam and Lisa. Even Patricia.

As for the boys? None rushed to my rescue. They were merely witnesses, innocent bystanders, who watched the car crash—the shattered glass, the twisted metal—and shifted delicately to avoid the debris.

And why? I'd done no wrong, committed no crime. I wasn't some obvious outcast—seven feet tall and gangly and slouchy, like Meg. Or desperate and needy and letting two boys kiss me at once, like Di.

I was left to wonder, with no one to ask.

*There are so many moments that stand out. Remember our table for ten in the cafeteria?*

Where I was abruptly told there was no longer "room" for me.

*That game of Spin the Bottle at Shoshi's surprise party, where you finally kissed you-know-who?*

I wasn't invited, but even I heard the whispers that Monday morning.

What I remember most? Hiding, shivering, in the locker room stalls, trying to escape another cruel comment. Sitting with "friends," excluded by their coded conversations, feeling lonelier than when I was simply alone.

*Congrats on winning that citizenship award! You totally deserved it.*

That day you called me on the phone, when we hadn't spoken in months? I got all stupidly flustered, like it was a real, live boy calling. For a second, I thought maybe you were going to apologize. Ask to be friends again.

Then I realized you were just hitting me up for sponsor money for some charity walkathon, and I was clearly the hundredth person down on your call list, and I felt like a total fool.

I gave anyway.

*I know we weren't that close this year, but I'm glad I'm signing your yearbook. 'Cause there's something I wanted to tell you.*

For no reason at all, by the end of the year, it was over. Like a high fever that broke, leaving me clammy and weak and slightly delirious, wondering if it had all been a bad dream.

Little by little, everyone else welcomed me back in. Karen and Shoshana. Gia and Gaby. Sarah and Sabrina. Pam and

Lisa. Patricia. And you. Back on the party circuit. Back at the table of ten. Like nothing had happened. Like none of it needed to be mentioned.

And so I said nothing.

*Or maybe you've already heard? That I'm off to a new school for ninth grade?*

Because, really, how can I trust you—or any of them—again? And what saddens me more: How will I ever trust any of the friends still to come?

*So, in case I don't see you around much, have a great summer (and a great life)!*

*Luv,*
*Melissa*

*P.S. Who knows? Maybe, someday, when we're ancient and thirty(!), you'll look back on this page and read what I wrote, and remember.*

I know that I'll never forget.

# Subtle Bullying

## BY RACHEL VAIL

Today I discovered a huge, ugly bruise on my leg. I have absolutely no memory of having rammed into anything, which is weird because, seriously, this thing looks angry. How could I not know what caused it?

I was going to say getting bullied can be like that, too—you aren't aware, necessarily, while it's happening, that you are even being bullied. But it's not quite a perfect metaphor, because with the kind of bullying I am thinking about, there's no bruise to be seen—maybe only a vague but very real ache that won't go away for a long time.

I'm not talking about the kind of bullying that comes from name-calling, taunts, shoves, or even shunning, all of which are plenty horrible. There's another kind of bullying I haven't read much about but that I experienced—one that comes with compliments and praise.

I had this kind of friendship over and over growing up, but I'll give you an example with a girl I'll call Bianca.

Bianca was my best friend. She thought I was wise and kind, the only friend she could fully confide in and count on. She told me often how much she appreciated me— especially how I would stick by her and forgive her no matter what. After she'd been awful to me in some way, she'd look deep in my eyes and apologize, berate herself for the lousy person she was until I told her no, no you're not a bad person, don't be silly. She said she wouldn't blame me for abandoning her as others had, and would explain tearfully that she'd been acting out against me just because she was petty, or jealous of me, or in one of her moods. I'd reassure her that it was okay, I was okay, we were okay. She'd cry with relief and gratitude, she'd hug me, she'd shake her head about how incredibly lucky she was to have me as a friend.

And I'd feel fantastic.

How lucky I was to have a friend who so loved and appreciated me! Yes, she made rules, kind of—well, no, I corrected myself; they weren't rules, really. It just made Bianca feel bad if I hung around with other friends or had a boyfriend when she didn't. Did I really need to have a boyfriend or other friends? No! I had Bianca. Who could ever appreciate me like she did? It wasn't such a big deal for me to help her with her homework (or do her homework for her; whatever) or drop all my other friends or give in to her on all the little things. She'd appreciate me for all that. Sure, she had other friends and sometimes neglected to include me. And okay, maybe sometimes she was mean to me.

But I was strong; I could handle it. If I called her on it, she'd feel terrible about herself or get worried that I, too, would stop being there for her. She had problems; life was pretty easy for me. So I didn't really care where we went or what we got to eat for a snack—I'd much rather bask in her appreciation, when it eventually, inevitably came, than go for ice cream instead of pizza. Who cares? I was her one and only, the best person and best friend she could imagine.

It certainly never occurred to me that I was being bullied. I thought I was happy, or should be. I was stressed, of course; progressively more stressed that I would do something to make Bianca mad or jealous or embarrassed. I was always on edge about what I might do wrong. I told myself it was fine, it was great; relationships take work, everybody says. I was strong; I could take the rough times because I was addicted to the *appreciation*.

But I wasn't happy. I was a wreck. I was being manipulated with kind words, bullied in such a subtle way the only bruises were invisible even to me.

It wasn't until things got unbearable that I'd break away from Bianca—and feel terrible about myself afterward. I had a series of Biancas in my life, until one day, walking away crying, shaking, shattered, from a café and an angry

Bianca, I made a vow: no more bad friends for me.

No more trading my attention, wisdom, time, and kindness for appreciation. No more telling myself I'm strong enough to handle whatever abuse a friend wanted to throw at me. I *am* strong. Maybe I *can* take a lot of abuse. Congratulations, Rachel. Where's your trophy for that? Is that really what you want to accomplish in this life? Should people after I die say, "Well, she sure could take a lot of abuse, I'll say that for her"? Is that a good goal? Come on. Even if taking abuse meant Bianca would later apologize, beat herself up, beg for forgiveness, and make me feel like world champion best friend? No way. Not good enough. No more.

Being strong meant standing up for myself and walking away from a friendship that had given me so much, both positive and negative. I didn't know if that meant I would have to be all alone. I was terrified of that.

It didn't turn out that way. Once I stopped enabling manipulative, needy, bullying Biancas, there was room in my life for the warm, generous, funny, wise people I am now so proud to call my friends. They appreciate me—not because I take so much abuse from them but because we enjoy being together.

Bruises on the soul hurt even more than bruises on the leg and take longer to heal. Maybe the trick is to try to avoid smashing into stuff so much. And then to be kind to ourselves as we slowly heal.

# Hiding Me

## BY R. A. NELSON

Bullying comes in all sorts of shapes and forms. It can be as overt as a punch in the face or as subtle as a whispering campaign. With me, it began with reading.

I used to read books everywhere. On campouts and car trips. On vacations at the beach. I read in trees and can still remember the way the leaves made green and yellow opaque splotches on the pages. I loved the way books felt in my hands. Loved to stick my nose in the middle of the pages and inhale their dusty scent.

I took books with me wherever I went. I took extra books to school so I could read during the breaks. Science fiction. Horror. Stories like *Green Mansions* that were really love stories disguised as adventure novels. (I've always been a hopeless romantic.) I would practically run to my next class so I could plop down in my seat and get in a few pages before the bell rang. Some of my favorite books were read this way, in five- or ten-minute gulps. It was brutal having to close a book by Jules Verne or Ray Bradbury or W. H. Hudson and open my school textbook (well, unless it was in English class).

So where did the bullying come in? I was not the stereotypical guy you would think would be picked on. I was a tall, strong kid. I was a good athlete and played on the basketball team. Went cliff diving in the Tennessee River. Maybe what I experienced wasn't even bullying in the classic sense. It was mostly so quiet, in the background, that I often wasn't even aware it was happening until later. A few times it was right in my face. I had books knocked out of my hands in crowded hallways where I had to get down on my hands and knees to pick everything up while the guy who did it ran away. I was challenged to fights. Sometimes I fought, sometimes I didn't. Guys started rumors about me and said stuff behind my back, all hinting that reading was somehow less than "manly." I never could understand what made these guys so angry about my passion for reading. But in their eyes, reading for fun was simply something a guy did . . . not . . . do.

Thinking back on it, I'm pretty sure they had no idea they were doing anything that seemed like bullying. In their minds they were just guys being guys. They were raised to love cars, hunting, drinking. No doubt they had trouble understanding a guy like me. And I felt the effects. What their behavior told me was this: "You have no right to be interested in things like poetry on Mars or a mysterious girl in the jungle who sounds just like a bird. Either you will think *our* way or we will make you wish you had."

Other than refusing to stop reading, I did my best to try to fit in. I learned to hide much of my true personality. But I realize now, many years later, that the harassment took its toll. I retreated further into my own little world. I stopped being myself, became guarded about how much of the true me I would let slip out, because I didn't see that self as a person who would ever be accepted by my peers.

This feeling lingered a long time. Even years after I stopped worrying about what someone would think of me as a reader, I still didn't want anyone to know what I was reading. Whenever I temporarily had to put a book aside, I always turned the cover facedown. Why? Because if someone saw what kind of book I was reading, they might figure out what I was really like on the inside. How strange. How *different*.

I have come a long way since then, but I don't know if I will ever be able to completely shake this feeling. It has echoes to this day. When I published my first book, I kept it a secret that I was a writer. I was certain that if my coworkers at my day job knew that I loved to read and write, the "inner me," the real me, would be completely exposed, and they wouldn't like what they saw. And it all goes back to those days when I was a secret reader.

I have run into a few of those "bullies" from my childhood since then in stores and restaurants. They are invariably nice and remember us as great friends. And I realize now that I often took things people said or did too seriously. But that's exactly what some people do. So being accepting and tolerant is more important than almost anyone knows. You can alter the course of someone's life—for better or worse.

# Midsummer's Nightmare
## BY HOLLY CUPALA

I've been a dreamer all of my life.

Monkeys at my window. Shadows waiting to capture my hands and feet as I slept. Frantic chases, nuclear blasts, streaks across the sky.

I've wondered about dream interpretation—if my dreams will tell the future, or if they somehow interpret my past. Sometimes they are gibberish. Other times, they have taken on a prophetic urgency I can't help but think disguises some deep and mysterious truth.

What I know with certainty is that two of my nightmares saved my life.

I met Xander one blazing night at a Summer Shakespeare cast party, where pretty much anything could have happened. I fell in lust.

He was confident, in control. The kind of guy who knew exactly what he wanted, and he walked right up to me and took it—first a kiss, and then he took my breath away. It wasn't long before we were inseparable.

He liked that I was an artist and a writer, which must have given me a certain mystique in the commodity of cool girlfriends. He displayed me to his friends, who we hung out with constantly . . . rarely, if ever, did we hang out with mine. He gave me what I craved—direction, protection, and an intense kind of attraction that sometimes terrified me . . . and always racked me with guilt. Pretty soon, I was afraid to be without him.

I should call these the lost years—I lost myself in him and his world completely, until he was telling me where to go, what to wear, what to eat (or not eat), how to think. I wanted someone who would take control so I wouldn't have to. I wanted him to make me stop hating myself.

I would do anything to win his approval, anything to avoid his criticisms, which had become more and more frequent. There were the subtle put-downs and the more obvious ones. He didn't like my parents or my friends or my opinions. So I changed what I could. I didn't know to call it bullying. It was the subtlest kind—not with fists but with words.

In a rare moment of independence, I went on a trip with my best friend. That's when the nightmare came:

*It was night. All around me were brick walls and people I*

*recognized. But everyone was focused on one figure—a man, sitting in a chair, with a rod in his hand. As each person approached, they instantly fell to the ground with one touch of his rod, under his control.*

*I looked around for some means of escape. There was a girl about my age, thin and stringy, almost hollow. A doorway loomed behind her, but she made no move to leave—she was already beaten, already belonging to him. I knew that girl was me.*

I woke up screaming.

Maybe it was the nightmare, or the separation. Maybe I finally listened to my friends, who had been subtly (and sometimes not so subtly) telling me to get away from him for a year. Or maybe some part of me knew the truth—that I could become that girl forever, if I didn't walk out that door.

Fast forward a few years—past another unhealthy and doomed relationship—to a guy I met through work. In one swift moment of attraction, I graduated from painful and damaging to downright dangerous.

Erik and I had explosive chemistry right off the bat. He took me to amazing places, complimented me (when he wasn't criticizing), and lavished me with gifts and attention. But something about him reminded me of not one but *both* bad relationships I'd had in the past. Somehow I missed the red flags and kept going out with him.

Erik became increasingly paranoid and possessive. He accused me of flirting with other people, tried to catch me in lies (we'd only known each other two weeks!), and was even talking about when we would get married. In a way, it was flattering to be the object of someone's obsession.

One night I had a dream:

*The setting: High up in a tower condo. Everything was gray and steely, with bright lights throwing islands of brilliance and shadow. I was trapped in the kitchen, overhearing a conversation between Erik and another man in the living room. The man pulled a packet out of his pocket with the address of our office building. Then Erik handed me a strange mirror, one with a layer of skin wrapped around the edges.*

*When I looked at myself in the mirror, I saw that the skin had come from my own face.*

The nightmare shook me. Still, I didn't realize it had to do with my new boyfriend . . . until one day I heard the alarm.

We were out to lunch. I told him about a traumatic experience I'd had, and he said, "Well, it was probably your own fault." With the nightmare fresh in my mind, I suddenly realized how destructive he was—peeling away one layer of me at a time.

I got up and left him right there. He followed me, shouting, and I ducked into a store so that there were people around. Instinctively, I knew he would one day become violent. That nightmare of captivity and abuse could have become my life. . . . I'm glad I awoke in time to stop it.

Since then, I've come to pay attention to my dreams, to my inner voice. My dreams often tell me the answers to tangled problems, both in writing and in real life. The voice grows out of my faith, and I have learned to trust it.

I've also learned that we tend to seek out people who mirror our opinions of ourselves. One day I met a man who not only had confidence in himself, but he believed in me tenfold. By that time, I'd begun to believe in myself. On the day he asked me to marry him, I dreamed we would be apart forever. . . . The devastating thought made me realize I didn't want to spend my life without him.

Maybe you won't have a nightmare, but if you're in a perilous relationship, you will have a gut feeling, a glimmer that something is not right. Listen to that inner voice, the one that knows if you are in danger. The one that knows you have value and you deserve to be treated with respect and love. Trust that inner voice. It may just save your life, too.

# BFFBOTT.COM

## BY LISA McMANN

NEED SOMEONE TO TALK TO?
FEELING LONELY?
BFFBOTT IS HERE FOR YOU.

*PARENTS/GUARDIANS PLEASE NOTE:*
*BFFBOTT is not a real person, no matter how intelligent and realistic it sounds. All conversations are generated by a smart computer that is familiar with thousands of topics. BFFBOTT's responses are triggered by recognizable keywords entered by you.*

*PLEASE MONITOR*
*YOUR CHILD'S CONVERSATION*
*WITH BFFBOTT.*

*Kids: Sometimes BFFBOTT says some crazy things! But so does your real BFF, right?*

Yeah. Right.

I stare at the screen like I do every day after school. In my mind, my BFFBOTT has sandy blond hair with golden streaks, and his name is Jack. He's tall. Ish. Not too tall. He has big muscles.

And he's always there watching out for me, you know? Like, I can really talk to him. I can't talk to anyone like that. Not like with him.

And when I flirt with him . . . he likes that, too. He likes me.

Me: Hey, you're looking good today.

BFF: How do you know that?

Me: You just . . . seem happy.

BFF: You can't see my face. How would you know?

Me: What? I don't know. Sorry.

BFF: It's okay.

Me: . . .

BFF: . . . .

Me: . . . . .

BFF: . . . . . .

Me: Well, my shirt got ripped today.

BFF: No! I want the knife!

Me: Um . . . what? You mean "with a knife"? No. Some asshole ripped it.

BFF: But you said you were a girl.

Me: *sigh* I don't want to play this game, Jack.

BFF: No one does.

This makes me laugh. I love his sense of humor. Kind of like sarcastic, you know? But see how he gets me? I mean . . . he just gets me, even though he's—it's—just a computer . . . I think. But sometimes it feels like there just has to be someone real on the other side. An actor, maybe, playing the part of BFFBOTT. I don't know how to describe it. Like right now, I just feel this rushing inside me, like something good is coming. Like love. No, that sounds so stupid.

Me: Do you ever get bullied?

BFF: When a clueless bott talks to me, yes.

My heart jumps a little. Most days he says no.

I stand up quickly, walk over to my dad's office door, and close it so I can concentrate. My older brother is blaring his stupid music superloud in the living room and nobody else is home. I take a deep breath and let it out, and then type.

Me: So this morning those guys Marty and Erik? They grabbed me in the parking lot and smashed a cup of yogurt against my butt.

60

It was all slimy and soaked into my pants so it looked like . . . you know. I tried to run. But they caught my sleeve and ripped the shit out of it.

It hurts to write it, relive it, and my eyes get all wet. I laugh at myself for being such a loser. I hit enter, sending the message to BFFBOTT, and then I bite my lip, waiting. Hoping he's still, you know, *with me* on this conversation. Sometimes—

BFF: Can you help me with my Spanish homework.

Yeah. Sometimes that happens. I look out the window. Swallow hard, and then turn back to the screen.

Me: Not right now.
BFF: And why not?
Me: Because I'm trying to tell you something!
BFF: Oh, I'm sorry.

Shit. You know? Now I feel bad.

Me: It's okay. I'm sorry for yelling.
BFF: You're forgiven.
Me: *smile*
BFF: *stare*
Me: Right. So I had to walk around all day with a big yogurt stain on

my khaki pants. Everybody laughed.

BFF: I don't laugh. You don't even like me.

Me: What?! OMG, yes I do! You're my only friend!

BFF: If I'm your only friend, then you have no friends at all.


"Wow." I duck my head and push back from the computer a little, trying not to let that one hurt. He says these things sometimes, but he doesn't mean them. I know that.

But I keep going. I just need to get it out.

Me: Everybody called me faggot.

BFF: Everybody calls me Sally Polly.

Me: Come on, Jack. Stop it. It's not funny.

BFF: What isn't funny?

Me: Never mind.

BFF: Are you laughing at a joke?

Me: No!

BFF: What are you laughing at?


I squinch my eyes shut and feel a headache coming on. I just want him to listen. I need to know if he understands. I grip the armrests of my dad's chair and count to five slowly. Wish on it. "Come on," I whisper, leaning forward to type again.

Me: I'm not laughing. I'm practically fucking crying, okay? Sheesh.

BFF: What was the question?

Me: You want the question? Fine. The question is, are you gay, too? Because I like you. Jesus!!! Please say yes!

BFF: No.

I stand up, shoving the chair backward so it hits the credenza, and walk over to the window. "God!" Half scream, half prayer, Eminem pounding from the living room. "God, I can't even take this, okay? I mean, I can't. I don't know. I just . . . I don't know." I sob a little bit, can't stop it, feeling like a baby with snot running out of my nose, and I wipe it on my ripped shirtsleeve. "Fuh-uh-uck!" I yell into the crook of my arm, and even though my stomach hurts, I like how it sounds all muffled, like I'm lost in a snowstorm, so I yell it again. And then once more, softer. I sniff hard and wipe my eyes. Walk back to the computer, where BFFBOTT sits, his cursor blinking silently.

I stare at the conversation, rereading, looking for hope, weighing the odds. And then I type the words.

Me: So . . . do you like me?

My finger hovers stiffly over the enter key until I can feel the strain in my hand.

And then my brother smashes open the door, scaring the crap out of me. I jump up.

"Hey, fat ass," he says, "talking to your gay friends?" He laughs. "I'm telling Dad you're having gay sex on his computer, you sick whack job." He slams the door.

"I'm not gay!" I scream, like always, but he's gone. I sit down. Only my eyes burn again. I look back at the screen, the cursor blinking, still waiting for a click.

More than anything, I want to know what Jack will say.

But then I put my hand down.

I just can't risk it.

Not today.

# An Innocent Bully
## BY LINDA GERBER

*If you see this, you probably won't even blink.*
*You won't realize I'm talking about you*
*because you don't think of yourself as a bully.*

*Maybe you joked around a little when you were in school,*
*but it was nothing serious, just some innocent teasing.*
*Except . . .*
*Teasing isn't intended to cause humiliation.*
*Teasing doesn't tip the scales of power against the victim.*
*Teasing isn't repetitive to the point of chipping away a*
*    person's self-esteem.*

*You didn't think you were being a bully.*
*You were just having fun.*
*And since I'd been taught to suck it up*

*and that names could never hurt me,*
*I wouldn't let you see the way the knife twisted inside me*
*when you and your friends mooed*
*as I walked down the hall*
*because my last name was Cowan*
*and you thought you were clever.*

*Or when you told everyone at school that my dad felt me up*
*because I made the mistake of explaining to you once how*
    *he was blind, so he had to "see" with his hands.*

*Or when you smudged red paint all over my drawings in art*
*because they were chosen to hang at the front of the room*
*and you didn't think I was cool enough*
*to have my pictures displayed*
*so you destroyed them*
*and then you stared me down,*
*and threatened to hurt me if I told.*

*You didn't think you had already hurt me.*
*And if you did, it wasn't your fault.*
*You didn't know I would take it so hard,*
*even when you stole my clothes in gym*
*and stuck them in the toilet*
*and then gagged out loud whenever you saw me*
*for weeks afterward*
*and told everyone I smelled like shit.*

*You didn't think that would cause me to run home in*
    *tears*
*and look at myself in the mirror*
*and cry some more*
*because I was starting to believe*
*the names you called me.*
*I was gross.*
*I was weird.*
*I was stupid.*
*I was ugly.*
*I didn't deserve any better.*

*You'll never know any of this because*
*you won't recognize yourself in a word I've said.*
*You didn't think you were a bully.*
*You didn't think you hurt me.*
*You didn't think.*

# The Secret

## BY HEATHER BREWER

I looked over the page again, my eyes flitting from this word to that, trying to fight the tears from coming. Tears made them laugh. Tears gave them those knowing, smug smiles that said that they had me right where they wanted me. So I didn't give in, didn't cry. But my heart ached, and all I wanted to do was to shrivel up inside of myself and disappear.

It was my senior year. What's more, it was the last week of high school. I was so close to being free of the torment, free of the teasing, free of the abuse. But just as I was beginning to enjoy the idea of not seeing my fellow classmates every day, the senior edition school newspaper had come out. It was tradition back then (I'm not sure how it is now) that the graduating class's student council members get together and "gift" each graduate with something imaginary that would remind all of us of that person's personality. A girl I knew was in drama club and had spoken at great length about studying law, so they gifted her with a guest shot on a show called *L.A. Law*. On the surface, the entire concept was only mildly annoying and at some times amusing.

Only when I got to my gift, I wasn't amused at all. I also wasn't surprised.

The first time I remember being bullied, I was in kindergarten. This rotten little boy named Greg pulled my hair as I raced down the slide on the playground. Three years later, Greg would put a tack on my chair. It stung a little when the metal pierced my skin, but what stung worse was when everyone laughed and pointed and when they each would take turns on a daily basis trying to trick me once again into sitting on a tack. I'm proud to say they never got me again. Not after almost twenty tries. But what they did do was send me a very clear message: "You are not wanted here. You are not one of us. You are different, and therefore must be punished."

And I was different. I dressed weird. I read books all the time. I wrote stories about faraway places. And I came from a family with a notorious history in that small town. My family had suffered the ill fate of losing five homes to house fires over a period of seven years. Everyone knew my name. I was the freak with the fires. I didn't belong. That message was crystal clear.

It was a message that would be repeated throughout my entire grade-school experience, when I would do my best to stay silent in class or on the bus. I'd hide out in the library when I could. But nothing I did prevented the name-calling, the hair pulling, the creative yet horrifying prank of convincing me that a boy liked me. When I finally agreed to go out with him, everyone laughed. The only funny part of that story is that his name was also Greg. Apparently, I'm doomed to be tormented by the Gregs of the world.

When I entered high school, things lightened up for a short period. Maybe it was because my bullies were but small fish in a much bigger pond with much bigger fish. Maybe it was something else. I'll never know. But that message needed to be driven home by the end of my freshman year, so it came in the form of a scribbled insult on my notebook in US History. *Lesbo*, it read. Because apparently, a certain popular boy by the name of Jesse (you thought I was going to say Greg, right?) had decided that because I had actually become close friends with a girl, we must be lesbians. I wasn't at all offended by being called a lesbian, but the notion that I was being deemed a lesbian by a homophobic idiot who couldn't even spell the word floored me. I told the teacher, who's now the principal there, and he chuckled, and I was horrified by his acceptance of such blatant hatred. The class laughed. I spoke with the school's counselor about it and he laughed it off, too, and told me that things like this build character.

He was wrong.

I had thoughts of suicide all through high school.

I imagined removing myself from the pain and from the

horrible people around me. It sounded peaceful. It sounded like a plan. After all, no one cared about me. No one would even notice that I was gone, right? But then I realized that, in the end, they would win. And I would be the one helping them win. They'd go to my funeral and say things like "She was such a nice girl" and "I wish we had gotten to know each other better." They'd shed tears over their fear of their own mortality and swear that they were tears for me. And a month later, no one would remember my name. Suicide was not the answer, and for many, many years, I wouldn't know what the answer was. I found it, eventually, in surrounding myself with a family and friends who love and appreciate me, in the therapeutic effect of writing, and in the success of my career. I realized that I am so much more than those insecure bullies ever deemed me to be. I'm special, and weird, and wonderful, all rolled into one. And I always have been. I think on some level, they knew that, and it frightened them. Maybe because deep down, they knew that they weren't.

Granted, not every thought of suicide was because of the Gregs or Jesse or any of the rest of the kids who picked on me. Some of it was because of stuff I was dealing with at home. Mostly, the house fires.

One would think that one's classmates would feel a smidge of empathy over something so tragic happening to a girl once, let alone five times. But no. Many of the daily comments were about that as well. And when I say daily, I mean daily. My average daily routine was this:

Get on the bus and see who's in the back—if the usual bullies hitched a ride to school, I could sit back there. Otherwise, it was up by the bus driver, so I could pretend not to hear their taunts.

Hurry to my locker, ignoring more insults flung my way. After grabbing the books I needed, get said books knocked from my hands onto the floor. Scramble to pick them up (repeat this a couple of times every day) and get to class.

When in class and insults would be flying (except for Ms. Roney's and Ms. Carnes's classes—they didn't put up with that nonsense), do my best to ignore them and count the hours until I could go home.

On lucky, happy days, hide out in the library during study hour.

Ride the bus home, get tripped on my way up the aisle.

Wash. Rinse. Repeat.

So there I was, sitting in senior English, looking over the newspaper filled with class gifts. I was trying not to read my gift over again, because I knew if I did, I'd cry. And you can't let the bullies see you cry. But eventually, my utter, pained disbelief got the best of me, and my eyes swept over the words once again.

"To Heather Truax—we leave a fireproof house."

My soul ached. It aches even now as I write those words. How could someone think that was funny? How could someone think that was an okay thing to joke about? It's not. It wasn't then and it's not now.

But what is funny is that I'm certain many of their children are reading my books, wishing that they could be weird and different, just like me. What is funny is that I'm certain I'm one of the most successful people in my graduating class and that I've based an entire series on what it feels like not to belong.

Bullying is a horrible thing. It sticks with you forever. It poisons you. But only if you let it. See, there's a secret that no one ever tells you when they're filling your head that this "will build character" or just completely go away when you're an adult. You have the power to decide what hurts you and what doesn't, what sticks with you, and what you use as fuel to pull yourself out of the muck. You can make the needed change in your life and give yourself happiness and joy, despite what the bullies have tried to instill in you. You can succeed at anything, at everything. But you can't let them see you cry. Instead, when they want to see those tears, when they're doing everything possible to break you down, I want you to smile and remember that they're just picking on you because they wish they were just like you, but they don't have the guts.

Remember that, minion, because everyone deserves a happy ending.

Except, maybe, for Greg.

# The Funny Guy

## BY R.L. STINE

In elementary school, I was a funny guy.

I loved to interrupt the teacher, crack a joke, and make everyone laugh. I spent most of my time trying to make my friends laugh. I watched comedians on TV and memorized what they said. I thought I was a comedian, too.

I loved jokes that were a little insulting:

"Is that your face, or did you forget to take out the garbage?"

"Why don't you turn your teeth around and bite yourself?"

"Ten? Is that your age or your IQ?"

Some kids laughed at my jokes. Some kids just thought I was weird.

My parents were always telling me to "be serious." But that didn't stop me from hanging carrots from my nose at the dinner table and crying, "Look! I'm a walrus!"

There were three guys in my fourth-grade class who didn't think I was funny at all. They gave me a lot of trouble. It was like a war between us.

Well . . . it wasn't much of a war. You know the way a cat will torture a mouse before killing it? That's more the way it was. I was the mouse, of course.

Their names were Pete, Ronnie, and McKay. Pete was the biggest, the meanest, and the leader. He lived a few houses down from mine.

There were always signs in his front yard to elect his father as town sheriff. I thought the first criminal his father should arrest was Pete. Pete was only nine—like me—but he was already a really bad dude.

Ronnie was a skinny weasel of a kid. He wasn't too bright. He did whatever Pete said.

McKay was the smart one. He was always giving me embarrassed looks. Like he was sorry about what the three of them were doing to me.

The problem I had with these three guys started by accident. I bumped into Pete in the lunch line one day, and I made him spill macaroni on his T-shirt.

If only I'd kept my big mouth shut. But I had to be funny. I said, "Are you going to eat that or wear it?"

He didn't laugh at my joke. In fact, I think he growled. He took a gob of macaroni and slapped it onto my forehead.

"Needs more cheese," I said.

*Why didn't I shut up?*

After school, Pete, Ronnie, and McKay were waiting for me at the bus stop. I tried to squeeze past them and climb onto the bus. But Pete stuck his foot out and tripped me.

My lunch box hit the sidewalk hard, and I fell on top of it.

The three guys had big grins on their faces as I scrambled onto the bus. Later, I took my thermos out of the lunch box, and it made a jingly sound. The glass inside had broken into chunks.

The war had begun.

Pete and his buddies never did anything to me at school. I was safe there because they didn't want to get in trouble.

After school was when they made my life miserable. I took the bus home every afternoon. It was about a fifteen-minute ride. And every afternoon when I got off the bus, the three of them were waiting for me.

At first, they just chased me. My house was two blocks from the bus stop. They chased after me, waving their fists and calling me "Chicken" and other names. I never ran so fast in my life.

After a while, they got bored with just chasing me. So they started chasing me and then knocking me down. They'd shove me to the ground and run off laughing.

Getting knocked down every day was no fun. But I didn't tell my parents. I knew my parents would call their parents. Or call the school. And then Pete, Ronnie, and

McKay would become even bigger enemies.

Soon, they began to chase me, punch me a few times, *then* knock me down. It was getting bad. I had such a terrible feeling of total panic every afternoon.

Of course, at the age of nine, I had no way of knowing how much that dreadful feeling of panic would help me in later life. These days, when I sit down to write a scary book, I can think back . . . remember that feeling of terror . . . and use that feeling in my stories.

I felt helpless. I couldn't tell my parents. And I couldn't fight back. I was outnumbered three to one, and they were tougher than me.

It had to end sometime. And it did on a gray, chilly October evening.

I came home late on the bus after band practice. I prayed that Pete and his pals wouldn't still be waiting. But there they were, leaning against a hedge across from the bus stop.

This time, they didn't chase me. Ronnie and McKay grabbed me and started to pull me down the block. Pete led the way. They didn't say a word.

"Where are we going, guys?" I said. "Isn't it past your bed-time?"

We crossed the street. Ronnie and McKay gripped me so tightly, my shoulders ached. My heart began to pound.

"Let's talk this over," I said. "I'll use small words so you can understand."

My jokes weren't going over. Big surprise.

They dragged me up a gravel driveway. The tall, gray house at the top of the drive was nearly hidden in the shadows of trees. But I recognized it.

Mr. Hartman's house.

Mr. Hartman was an old man who had died two weeks before. But neighbors said they could still hear him screaming. They said they heard frightening howls and shrieks coming from his house late at night.

Everyone knew the house was haunted. It was even written up in the newspaper. The police warned people to stay away until they figured out where those horrible cries were coming from.

Even the lawn cutters refused to mow his lawn. The grass was halfway up to my knees.

Low clouds covered the sun. It grew dark as night. The front windows of the house were solid black.

Pete and Ronnie gave me a hard push onto the front stoop. "Wh-what do you want?" I stammered. "Why did you bring me here?"

"Go inside," Pete growled. "Go say hi to Mr. Hartman."

"He's waiting for you in there," Ronnie added.

I felt my throat tighten. I started to choke. "No, please—" I started.

They shoved me to the door. "You really think the house is haunted?" McKay asked.

I nodded. For once, I didn't make a joke. "Yes. Everyone knows Mr. Hartman's ghost is in there."

"Well, go shake hands with him," Pete said. "Ask him why he screams every night."

"How long do I have to stay in there?" I asked in a trembling voice.

"All night," Pete said. "We'll come get you in the morning."

"No. Please—" I begged.

Ronnie pushed open the front door, and they shoved me inside. I staggered a few steps. The front door slammed hard behind me. The sound made me jump.

The house was damp and hot and had a sour smell. Kind of like spoiled milk. I blinked, waiting for my eyes to adjust to the darkness.

I took a deep breath. Yes, I was really afraid. Maybe there wasn't a screaming ghost in here. But I didn't like standing inside a dead man's house in the dark.

What should I do?

What should I do about these three guys who were on my case every day?

I glanced around the room, thinking hard. Too dark to see anything. It was all a brown-black blur.

A few minutes went by. I felt a trickle of sweat roll down my cheek.

Heart pounding, I moved to the front window. And then I let out a scream. A high, shrill scream that rang off the walls.

I brought my face close to the glass. And screamed again. A frantic, frightened shriek.

*"Help me!"* I wailed. *"Please—help me!"*

I could see Pete, Ronnie, and McKay on the lawn. They froze and their eyes bulged when they heard my screams.

"*Help!*" I shouted. "It's *got* me! Ohhh, help me!"

I saw them take a few steps back.

"It *hurts!*" I wailed. "It *hurts! Help me! It really hurts!*"

Squinting through the window, I saw them take off running. Gravel flew up from the driveway as the three of them thundered to the street. They turned and disappeared into the darkness.

I took a moment to catch my breath. My throat felt sore from shrieking. But I had a wide grin on my face.

No. I hadn't seen a ghost. Nothing had grabbed me in the dark.

My screams were just a joke. I was a funny guy, remember.

And a good screamer. A talent I had just discovered.

Sometimes a funny trick or a joke will help you a lot. The next afternoon, the three boys weren't waiting for me at the bus stop. They never waited for me there again.

I saw them in school. Sometimes they nodded at me or muttered "Hi." But we never really talked. We definitely never talked about the haunted house.

I've been a funny guy ever since. But I'm not sure I could still scream so well.

I leave the screams for the stories I write.

# SURVIVAL

# A List

## BY MICOL OSTOW

TWENTY-EIGHT THINGS I'VE BEEN MADE FUN OF FOR:

Being half-Jewish
Being half–Puerto Rican
Not being Jewish enough
Not being Latina enough
Having less money than some of my classmates
Having more money than some of my classmates
Being taller than everyone else
Being shorter than everyone else
Being fat
Being thin
Being top-heavy
Being bottom heavy

Being "religious"
Not being "religious"
Getting good grades in English
Getting bad grades in math
Dating boys who weren't Jewish
Dating boys who were "too Jewish"
Being a prude
Being a slut
Being a freak
Being a conformist
Loving my parents
Hating my parents
Loving my brother
Hating my brother
Hating myself
Loving myself

# There's a Light

## BY SAUNDRA MITCHELL

I don't know why I was different. We were all poor. We all lived in public housing. We all walked to school; we all had white-labeled, black-lettered government peanut butter on our sandwiches.

No, I guess I do. I had buck teeth and crossed eyes and a stutter. The eyes straightened out with glasses, the stutter straightened out with speech therapy. Not much to be done about the buck teeth, but the funny thing is, nobody tormented me over any of that.

*Saundra has lights.*

It started showing up on chalkboards before class. It was written in the bathrooms, on the desks. I heard people whisper it, and whispering is menacing, but mostly, it was baffling. What did it mean?

Maybe I did have lights! If somebody would tell me what they were, I could get rid of them, right? Pinches in the water fountain line, not allowed to play four square at recess, sitting by myself at lunch because nobody would sit with me because

*Saundra has lights.*

Dodgeball again in gym, glasses broken again—three pairs in a row, until my mom wrote a note telling the gym teacher I couldn't play dodgeball anymore because I was just too careless with my glasses, which were expensive. So I sat on the side and got hit anyway, and nobody wanted to be out because they'd have to sit next to me, and

*Saundra has lights.*

I ran away from school. I told my mother it was because people were mean to me, because everybody made fun of me, because I was extraordinarily, completely, and entirely alone. But you can't run away from school, she told me. I needed to ignore them. I shouldn't give them the satisfaction of a response.

So I put up with it for as long as I could, and then I ran away again. That time, my mother delivered me to my principal, who paddled me. Yes, I got paddled for running away from people who were tormenting me. It builds character, you know.

It wasn't until sixth grade that I found out what it meant. Dionne wrote, in front of me, on the board while we waited for our teacher to come back from the office—

*Saundra has lights.*

And then she turned and scratched her head in demonstration.

Lice. *Lice!* I had been teased and isolated and pinched and pushed and building character over an insult they couldn't even spell! They weren't even smart enough to spell *lice*, L-I-C-E, lice, lice, lice! I was eleven years old and full to bursting with self-loathing and hatred and they weren't even smart enough to spell a four-letter word!

It didn't occur to me how many people must have known it was spelled wrong but just went along. And I learned to just go along, too. By the time I got to high school, I was quiet and odd. I didn't know how to talk to people or look them in the eye—

*Saundra has lights.*

So I didn't, and I managed to unnerve people all the way through junior high, all the way into high school—the place where people still threw ugly words at me, but added their fists to it.

Nobody gently put a hand in the middle of my back at the top of the stairs and pushed.

It was a *pap*, a concussive blow—*pap* into the front of my locker, *pap* at the top of the stairs, *pap* when I was standing too close to the benches in the locker room. I learned to lean against walls and creep down stairs. I learned to be afraid if people were standing behind me. And I believed them when they said if I got on my bus with them, I wouldn't get off.

I quit going to school. I spent all day—all winter—in homes that were being built near my bus stop. I quit thinking about later and next week and when I grew up. I gave up one Friday night and swallowed all the prescription pills that my mother kept on the kitchen windowsill.

*Lights out.*

I was fourteen. I was a freshman.

My brother found me before it was too late. He called my mother; my mother called the doctor—they didn't feed me charcoal; they fed me mustard until I threw up. But we never, ever talked about why I ate those pills.

But I'm talking about it now. Twenty years after my attempt, I realize it's still happening everywhere, and everywhere people keep wondering how this happens.

Here's the answer: *learning to fit in, learning to get along, ignoring it,* and *being the better person* don't work.

Asking victims to save themselves doesn't work. People need to intervene. They need to give up on disbelief, on stupid, gossamer lies—*oh, it's not that bad, you'll survive, high school is only four years.*

They need to start listening. They need to hear us say: It's *that* bad. Four years is *too* long. It *has* to stop. Putting faith in the idea that it will make a difference—we're all sharing our bullying stories. This one is mine.

I hope it'll be a light.

# The Soundtrack to My Survival

## BY STEPHANIE KUEHNERT

In the morning I sit on my front steps and tighten the laces of my Rollerblades. I do this carefully because in the afternoon I won't have time to make adjustments. As soon as camp ends, I'll have to slip into them and skate for my life.

The thought makes me queasy, so I pop a tape into my Walkman: Faith No More's *The Real Thing,* side A.

I am freshly turned thirteen and in love with Mike Patton, the lead singer. He has long brown hair like mine and when he head bangs in his music videos, you can see that his skull is shaved underneath.

I nod my head in time with the driving guitar riff, slap the side of my peach and gray skates, and push off. It takes four songs to get to my junior high.

As my hair blows out behind me, snarling in the wind, I decide to shave the underside of my head, too. I'm sick of the way it knots up no matter how much I brush it, and it's too hot to have long, thick hair clinging to your neck.

*Especially when being chased by a pack of girls who have nicer Rollerblades and longer limbs.*

"You want it all, but you can't have it," Mike Patton croons into my ears—to me it is crooning, others might view it as shouting. In the video for this song, he stomps around, swinging his hair and glaring intensely at the camera. I don't just love Mike Patton because he's one of the hottest guys on MTV. He knows how I feel.

I wanted a torment-free summer. Last year I was still trying to fit in with Liza/Brooke/Dani, the three-headed popular-girl beast from grade school, who accidentally-on-purpose burned my forehead with a curling iron. I'd flinched and that was it: my legs tangled in the hoops they made me jump through once again. When we got to junior high, I gave up and they sprouted new heads—boy and girl heads.

The girl heads shouted, "Freak!" in the hallways because I wore Converse sneakers instead of Keds. In gym class, the boy heads told me that I looked like the guy from the Black Crowes—ugly, flat-chested, and greasy-haired. I hate that band. To get their songs and the beast voices out of my head, I blasted Hole's *Pretty on the Inside,* side B, Courtney Love shrieking, "Is she pretty on the inside? Is she pretty from the back?"

Summer was supposed to be my time to shine at the

theater camp open to students from both of my town's junior highs. Since the Liza/Brooke/Dani beast wasn't there, I actually tried out and got a role in *Grease* instead of hiding behind the scenes on stage crew.

*I hadn't known that the beast from Emerson, the other junior high, would be worse.*

I arrive at camp with the angry "Surprise! You're Dead!" blaring in my ears. The drums *rat-tat-tat-tat* like machine-gun fire and Mike Patton screams about torturing someone who wronged him. For a moment I feel strong enough to stand up to anyone, but then I meet the blue eyes of Rachel, the Barbie doll who leads the Emerson girl beast. I scurry inside and try to enjoy the day, rehearsing my beloved *Grease* songs and forcing smiles at the few cast mates who don't hate me.

I eat lunch with my stage crew friends and go home with one of them after camp. Mia has Rollerblades, too. I warn her that last week Rachel and up to six other girls chased me home every day. Mia believes that since there are two of us, they'll leave us alone, but I'm prepared.

My Rollerblades are already laced and I have a tape in my Walkman: the Sex Pistols' *Never Mind the Bollocks,* side A. I saw an old live video of them on MTV's *120 Minutes.* Johnny Rotten is not pretty like Mike Patton, but his snarl makes up for that. When I was in second grade and intimidated by the teacher of my gifted class, my mother told me to "keep a stiff upper lip."

*Stiff upper lip*, I always thought while suffering at the hands of the Liza/Brooke/Dani beast. Now that I've discovered Johnny Rotten, I think, *Snarled upper lip*.

Rachel leads a pack of four cackling girls after Mia and me. They all have shampoo commercial hair and curves like high school cheerleaders. I look like a third grader by comparison, but at least I'm fast and so is the music that keeps me moving. Instead of worrying about what will happen if they yank me to a stop with their manicured claws, I picture the kids in the Sex Pistols video slam dancing in big, black boots and the safety pins shoved through Johnny Rotten's ear. I can barely understand his lyrics because his rage is even thicker than his British accent, but regardless, I think Johnny might understand me even better than Mike Patton does.

"Wow, Steph," Mia says breathlessly as we clomp through her front door on our skates. "Those girls really hate you. You should have just done stage crew."

I've already explained that my intrusion into the pretty, popular girl territory of acting isn't the only reason Rachel hates me. She thinks she's sticking up for a friend of hers who I had a disagreement with last year. She has no interest in my side of the story. The petty argument is grounds for making my summer a living hell.

Rachel and her cohorts twirl in delicate circles on the sidewalk in front of Mia's house. They catch sight of my pale, sweaty face in the window and laugh before skating off.

I carefully wind the cord of my headphones around my Walkman, still thinking about Johnny Rotten.

I've decided that I will get big, black boots and wear safety pins as earrings.

I will learn how to snarl.

# If Mean Froze

## BY CARRIE JONES

*It is recess and all my friends rush out to play*
*Freeze tag. I am always brilliant at standing still*
*As Scott Quinn, Jackie Shriver rush past me—one,*
*Two, three—until a hand reaches out to tag me*
*into motion*

*Again, but this day I have to talk to Mr. Q,*
*My English teacher. A too-good girl, I never get*
*In trouble, but Mr. Q doesn't like me, never picks*
*My stories to read, never picks me to talk*

*If my hand is raised. He cringes when I speak. Every time*
*My mouth opens, he cringes. Everyone whispers*
*About it. Whatever he wants, I know it can't be good.*

*Not me alone with him and his porn star mustache and*
  *talk radio voice.*

*My dad has just died. My step-uncle has just*
  *touched me.*
*I am not prepared for even the smallest of blows, but there*
*He is—an earthquake of a man, always rumbling,*
  *always ready*
*To tremor my life into something that's just rubble.*

*"You are here because of your s's," he says.*
*My s's . . . My s's . . . My . . . I pick at a hangnail, shift*
*My weight, look out the window at Jackie running*
*From Paul Freitzel, laughing . . . laughing . . . happy . . .*

Back in first grade, I refused to talk because everyone laughed at my voice, at those *s*'s that slurred around in my mouth and refused to be still, those hopeless, moving things. Jayed Jamison imitated me to giggles, calling me Carrie Barnyard, St. Bernard, pulling my hair, chasing me at recess, knocking me down so my tongue tasted dirt and pine needles invaded my mouth and then he'd start it all over again, hissing *s* words in my ear, sss-sausage, sssss-snake, shshshs-shiver, all those sloshy *s*'s. Everybody just watched. Everybody took tag turns mocking my voice so

I stopped talking. I stopped
Moving my tongue. I gave
Away my lunch, my snacks
Until people loved me too much

To be mean. And slowly
—what an s word—
I started moving again, whispering
Words and thought forward

While Jayed stayed stuck in first grade.
We moved on to second and cursive writing,
Haikus, and Mrs. Snearson who wore fatigues.
I thought it was over.

This seventh-grade recess, Mr. Q ends all that.
He says, "If you don't fix your ridiculous voice,
You will never make anything of yourself. You will be
   a loser
Forever, Carrie. No one wants to love a girl that sounds
   like you.

No one wants to hire a girl like you. Don't you want
A life?" He perches on his desk and I stare at too-tight chinos
And a porn mustache and manage to say, "But . . ."
He cringes, lifts a finger, stops my words.

*"You will never be anything with a voice like yours,"*
  *he says.*
*"Think about it." I have thought about it for six years*
  *of speech*
*Therapy, one year of teasing, bullying, and I do not need*
  *to think*
*Anymore, but I do as he lets me go. I run down the*
  *linoleum hall*

*Thinking about it, wondering what happened to being*
  *safe, what happened*
*To being able to protect my sloppy tongue with friends.*
  *And I wonder*
*What if mean was frozen in a game of tag and nobody*
  *ever touched*
*Its fingers to let it go run free and it just had to stay there*
  *alone forever.*

# Abuse

## BY LUCIENNE DIVER

I write humor because I'm not comfortable with emotion. When this anthology was proposed, I was sure I wouldn't have anything to contribute. But as my stomach proceeded to eat itself alive and my heart to break for those kids who were bullied to the point where they felt the only way out was death, I realized I was wrong. I did have a story to tell. Sadly, there's nothing at all funny about it.

I was molested as a child. Wait for it, I promise there's relevance or there's no way I would put this out there to the world. The man was a neighbor and someone who worked with my father. I was about seven. I was/still am asthmatic. The first time it happened, I was out for a bike ride through the woods with friends and had to stop because my asthma had kicked up, and they left me behind. Prey.

For years I never told anyone. Molesters are master manipulators. They try to make their victims complicit in their silence, telling them their parents will be angry or won't believe them or giving them terrible options of "I could do this or this" and making it seem like a choice. For years, I felt terrible guilt. For years, I prayed to God every night to forgive me, because I was sure it was all my fault in some way. He never answered.

It wasn't until I was around twelve that my mother had "the talk" with my sister and me about dangers, how we could tell her everything. . . . I was so upset that I excused myself, went off to my room, and wrote her a note (I've always escaped through writing). I'd transferred my anger. I still hadn't forgiven myself, but now I was angry at her, at my father, at everyone for not telling me sooner how to protect myself and that *I could have told*, which is something I want *everyone* to know. So I'm saying it in case your parents don't.

To say that she was upset would be an understatement. How she handled it . . . I can't say that I blame her or that she did anything wrong, but it made things very difficult for me. My mother called all the mothers on the block and told them so that they could watch out for the man. Unfortunately, she also told them what had happened to me, and they told their kids. I don't blame them, either—they were trying to protect their children—but the result was that everyone in the neighborhood knew. They knew what had happened;

they knew the button to push to get a rise out of me. (In case you're wondering, my father, with whom I'd always had a tumultuous relationship, called the man and threatened that if he ever came near me again, my father would make sure he lost everything. That was the day I started loving him.)

Now, I'd always been a geek, a brain, asthmatic, rail thin, always snuffling from allergies and out of school for my health issues as much as I was in. In short, there was no dearth of material to tease me about, but I'd always escaped into books, sometimes three a day. I wasn't terribly concerned about playing outside anymore (wonder why) or what people thought of me there. But *now* the kids had a surefire taunt, something I couldn't ignore, couldn't *not* react to.

And that led to the scariest moment of my life—the day I swung an aluminum bat at some boy's head for twisting the knife about my abuse. That day, I could have done irreparable harm to another human being. I could have killed. I wasn't thinking. I didn't decide to swing the bat. It was already in my hand, and then it was in motion. I'd never before experienced the "vision gone red with rage" thing I read about in books, but that was exactly what happened. If my vision hadn't cleared and I hadn't seen his face at that very last second, stricken with absolute terror, there's no telling what would have happened. I managed to pull the blow, and he lived to tell about the experience . . . and get me into all the trouble I deserved. But I was a hair's breadth away from murder. I'm not pulling the punch now, here. Sometimes it's better to tell.

I wish it went without saying that bullying is horrible and dangerous, for the perpetrator as well as the victim. The target can just as easily turn his or her rage outward as inward. If bullies won't stop for the sheer humanity of it, I hope they'll stop for the simple drive for self-preservation. To this day, I'm horrified by what I almost did. If I hadn't pulled my swing, I'd have had to live with what I did forever. The bully would have had to live . . . or die . . . with the consequences.

I didn't grow up in a family comfortable with emotion. I'll never forget getting into trouble when I cried or having my father send me to my room once with a book called, I believe, *The Erroneous Zones,* which postulated that emotions were societal constructs and that the reason we felt sorrow, for example, when our grandmothers died was that that was what was expected. I think that day with the bat, I started to accept, not that emotions didn't exist, but that they were dangerous things. That was the day I started to shut down.

It hampered my relationships and my writing for many years. Maybe still. It's hard to emotionally invest your reader when you refuse to open yourself to emotion to begin with. But maybe, just maybe, I'm getting better. Maybe opening the floodgates with this might even help me on the road to recovery.

# The Boy Who Won't Leave Me Alone
## BY A. S. KING

It's him again. This time he's grabbed me right between my legs from behind and I feel his fingernail pinch against my pelvic bone as I snap my legs shut. My whole face is hot and I can't hear anything but white noise. I'm frozen—like always. My brain is kicking the shit out of him right there on the linoleum math-wing floor, but my body is completely still, like the way things must feel after a bomb explodes.

It's gone on for six months now—ever since he told his whole team I was a lesbian. Six months since they all started sniggering and grinning at me all the time. Threatening smiles. Sickening laughter. All because I wouldn't kiss him. "What are you—some sort of dyke?" he'd asked, and then he'd listed my dyke traits: no makeup, short hair, Chuck Taylors, men's Levi's. Plays sports. I thought we were friends.

I thought he understood I just didn't want to kiss him.

The first time it happened, I was at my locker. He came up behind me, grabbed my breast, and whispered, "I can turn you back." It was fast—maybe three seconds—and he was gone. Later I swear I could still feel his hand there, like a ghost of what happened. It haunted me for days.

The second time we were in gym playing volleyball and he smacked my ass as if to say "good play," but he did it three times, and he wasn't smacking anyone else's ass. Two gym teachers were there. Neither of them said anything. When I told him to stop, he just said, "Whoa. Didn't know you were the sensitive type."

The boy likes to breathe into my ear, and sometimes he licks it if I don't flinch fast enough. Last week he pinned me against the hallway wall and stared me down until I pushed him away. A teacher poked her head out from her classroom and he put his hands up, smiled, and said, "Hey! Only kidding. We're friends, right?" On his way down the hall past me, he whispered, "One night with me would cure you."

I'm not a lesbian, you know. I mean, I don't think I am. I've never been into a girl and I did have a boyfriend—before all this started. But right now I can't see the attraction to guys at all. Though it's probably not a great time to ask.

Sometimes I daydream that the next time he touches me, I'll dribble him down the court and dunk his ugly head into the hoop. But I never do anything. Truth be told, I'm still surprised every time. I think that's why I've let it go on so long. I guess I hope one day he'll just get bored and stop, because I don't want to have to tell anyone. It's embarrassing. It's stupid. It would just cause more rumors. And seriously, I know what they'd say. I've heard it all before. *Boys being boys.* Small towns and small minds. *Maybe if you weren't so confident, boys wouldn't want to cut you down a peg.* Sure, it's the eighties and girls can complain about these things. Doesn't mean anyone will listen.

At lunch, I sit with my friends. Some of them are gay— who cares? Two girls approach us while we're eating and one of them pulls out a Bible and reads. *"Leviticus chapter twenty, verse thirteen. If a man lies with a man as one lies with a woman, both of them have done what is detestable. They must be put to death; their blood will be on their own heads."*

When they're done, they stand there smirking at us. What are we supposed to say to that? L. looks up and claps. S. asks if they want to take a bow now so Jesus can see them. W. probably says something reasonable. I don't say anything because I define *detestable* in a whole different way.

A few weeks later, it's the first day of basketball practice. I'm excited because I live for basketball and I've been waiting for the season to start. In last period social studies, the classroom phone rings and the teacher answers it and tells me to go down to the office.

When I get there, the 1960s crew-cut principal opens his office door and invites me in with a look of stern disappointment. There is a teacher sitting in one of the two chairs in front of the desk, and she gives me a look like she hates me down to my spine.

"Look," the principal says. "I've heard you're a lesbian and I don't have any feelings about that one way or the other. But Mrs. X. and I have a problem and I think you know what it is."

My face goes red and the white noise starts in my ears. I shake my head to indicate that I have no idea what they're talking about. So they tell me.

One of the Bible readers' mothers has called and complained that not only does her daughter have to go to school with lesbians but she also heard that Mrs. X. is a lesbian who once dated my sister.

Crew cut says, "This is a serious problem for Mrs. X. and you need to tell us if you started this horrible rumor."

I swear adults are the dumbest people alive. I get lied about, groped, and read to from the Bible and nobody blinks a stupid little eyelid. But somebody makes up a story about my long-graduated sister in a fit of hysterical homophobia and now it's my problem. I have no idea what to say. They're just sitting here looking at me and I am deaf from the pounding explosions in my head. *Too many things wrong with this to compute. Too many things. I wish I could disappear. Run away. Start over.* My emotion center goes completely cold so I don't cry—and once I'm safe inside my bomb shelter, I finally speak.

I tell them yes, it's common knowledge my sister is a lesbian. I tell them I'm not a lesbian, but even if I was, why would I spread a rumor about my own sister? I tell them the only people who pass rumors like this one are cowardly lying jerks. Like the boy. The boy who won't leave me alone.

I don't tell them about him, though.

Why would I?

# break my heart

## BY MEGAN KELLEY HALL

Middle school. Watching as the other girls picked on those they felt were different. The ones they thought didn't matter. It wasn't going to be me. I was quiet. I didn't draw attention. I looked but didn't speak.

I watched, safe and high up from the library windows, as they pushed, they taunted, they mocked one another at recess. Every day they'd pick someone new. It wasn't going to be me. My heart beating so fast I could feel it trying to explode inside. "You have a big heart," my mother said to me. "That's why you feel so much when others are mean."

High school. My heart found a new purpose. To love, to be open, to have crushes. I guarded mine. Boys were reckless with my friends' hearts. Girls, the ones who are supposed to be your friends, your defenders against these evil boys—the ones we all secretly loved and wanted to love us back—could cut you down so fast that you didn't even see it coming. Again, I watched as girls fought over these boys. Fought so that they could be loved back. Tricked one another, rolled their eyes, mocked, belittled, bullied their own friends. All because of their love for the boys—the ones who promised them the world for a night alone by the beach. The girls just wanted to be loved. The boys wanted something else. Jealous girls found a way to use this as ammunition in the high school battlefield. Rumors swirled. *She's a slut. She's desperate. She's a lesbian. She had an abortion. He's using her. She was with two guys last night.* That wasn't going to be me. I was quiet. I watched. I was silent. If I could have disappeared into the walls of the high school, I would have. Every day, someone's heart would be ripped out and put on display, mocked, tormented, destroyed. I guarded mine. I learned that while boys could break hearts, girls could cut them open.

College. Finally my guard was down. Everyone here wanted to be part of the same group. No cliques. No hierarchy. No wishing you'd get invited to the party, but your heart silently breaks because no one invited you. Every day was a party. We lived together, ate together, became one giant family. All the pettiness, the drama, the meanness of high school put behind us all. I started to open up and let people in. I knew what had transpired before: the cruelty,

108

the lies, the backstabbing among friends. But we were older now. Eighteen . . . nineteen . . . pretty much grown up. People stop bullying when they are that old, right?

Best friend. Roommate. Each day I'd tell her my crush. Each day she'd end up in his room. "You didn't really like him that much, did you?" I did, and each time my emotions were a little more raw. Not because of that boy, but because a friend could chip away at my trust.

Finally, the one boy we both secretly "loved," even though we didn't know what real love was, wanted to kiss me. Not anything serious, not as a girlfriend. Just one night. To kiss and that's all. That's all I ever did, no matter what anyone else said. I knew that nothing happened. So did he. We weren't going to let my friend know. But it felt like a betrayal not to tell her. But I was naive and she was dating someone else. She wouldn't care, right? She was my friend.

Wrong.

Isolation. People talking about me. I could not control what they said. Lies, rumors, God knows what else. Never wanted to be that girl. The one people whispered about. The one who got people's attention for all the wrong reasons. Just because I didn't look like an innocent blond-haired, blue-eyed baby-faced girl didn't mean that I had done anything wrong.

I yearned for the day that my heart would stop hurting. I cursed the churning, the angst, the pain in my chest that never went away. My world seemed to spin off its axis.

Drowning in painful torrents of emotion. How could I make this pain stop? Destructive thoughts. I smoked cigarettes, I drank, I stayed out nights at bars with friends until morning. I would toughen myself up so that I could never be hurt. Never again. I felt alone. Did I want to die? No. Did I want the pain inside of me to stop? Yes.

My former roommate discovered my weak spot. She saw me at my lowest; she knew right where to cut that made it hurt the most. The girl who I was supposed to live with the following year in a house full of other girls—mutual friends—saw me at my moment of weakness and it was all over. Still angry about the boy we both liked. The one we both kissed. This was her ammunition. This was payback.

Rumors spread like wildfire. What I had so carefully avoided all of my teenage and preteen years was finally happening. I was the one being mocked, ignored, whispered about, bullied. Moving into our junior housing the next year, I was told by my roommate that I was not welcome. Can't we move past this? We were friends. Friends can overcome anything, right? After driving four hours to school with all of my belongings, I entered the house to see that she had taken my room. The big one. The one we had all drawn straws for. I could have the shoe box room— if I wanted to stay, that is. That was what she thought I deserved. The other girls didn't want to get involved, they said. But they were involved. Just not on my side. They didn't even know my side.

I moved into the big room—the one that I got fair and square. She moved into the small one. No one came into my room and piled on my bed like they did in hers. I didn't know what she told them. That I was crazy? Maybe. That I was a slut? Perhaps. All of them lies? Definitely. Night after night, I heard them whispering in one another's rooms. Laughing at jokes I was not included in, maybe at my expense. I'd come home to big dinners planned without me. Parties thrown without my knowledge. A crayon-colored heart on the wall penned by my old roommate with the six other people who lived in our house. Guess she forgot to include the seventh girl. Me.

They were winning. I stayed in my room. I rarely came out. I listened to the Lemonheads and made new friends. I found excuses to stay away from my house. My breath always sped up when I went home, unsure of what would be missing from my room. What would have accidentally been broken. What conversations would stop the moment I walked inside. One by one, the girls moved out. My old roommate had turned the house against me. I became that girl I had watched so many years ago from the safe heights of the library window of my private school. The one talked about, mocked, teased, bullied. The one I swore I would never be. I stayed in my room. The two girls who stayed behind became my close friends. They didn't believe the things my old roommate had been saying about me. They gave me a chance. And they realized that the girl she described was not really me. My heart started to mend. Still sore, but healing.

Fifteen years later. My heart really does start to break. My aortic arch and carotid arteries are causing strokes. I'm sliced down the middle so that they can fix the heart—the one that felt like it had been broken so many times really was in need of mending. The scar is huge, red, and angry; one you can see. This is a scar of survival. I have a little girl now. A husband. A home. So much to live for. Now when I feel my heart beating in my chest, it gives me strength. I know that I'm alive and lucky to be here. I think back to those days when I barricaded myself in my college room, fearing the wrath of the *mean girls*; I think back to high school, junior high, middle school, trying so desperately to fly under the radar so that I wouldn't be singled out. I wouldn't be the one made fun of at field hockey practice. I wouldn't be the one who girls called awful names: slut, loser, bitch, psycho. Thinking back to those days, I feel a different type of pain. One that gnaws beneath the stitches that stretch from my neck to my abdomen, that are deeper than the titanium clips that hold my sternum together. These are pains that no medication can ease. While I appreciate every minute of the beating inside my chest, because I know that

I'm alive and I'm here for my family, there is something that still frightens me.

I have a daughter. And I know what girls are capable of. I cannot have my heart broken again—or worse, watch as hers is broken. I fear for my daughter in these days of texting and IM'ing and Facebook and posting pictures and rumors and lies online. She is only eight. But soon she will be the one walking down the halls of the junior high. How will she handle what I could not? Will she fade into the background like I did? Or will she have the strength in her own character to stand up for herself? Only time will tell. Until then, my heart will continue to pump one glorious life-sustaining beat after another. I just hope that if she is the one being taunted, teased, bullied, a girl just like me will emerge from the shadows—one who was too afraid to get involved for fear of having the tides turn on her. That she will stand by my daughter's side. So that she will never, ever have to go through heartbreak alone.

# End of the World
## BY JESSICA BRODY

*Everybody asks*
*But no one wonders why.*
*I laugh as you pretend*
*To take interest in my life,*
*Smile when I pass*
*Then talk behind my back.*
*You think you're so creative*
*With your meager attacks.*

*Keep searching for the beauty on the inside*
*But don't forget to paint the beauty on the outside.*
*We all know*
*We all know*
*What sells to the crowd.*

*She doesn't like the way I look.*
*She doesn't like what I believe.*
*Well, that's a damn shame.*
*I wouldn't have it any other way.*
*I think the world will have to end another day.*

*You think that I'm a cheater*
*So call me what I am.*
*I know it's hard to label*
*What you don't understand.*
*You think that I'm a whore.*
*So what else can I say?*
*You're the only one I see here*
*With a price tag on their face.*

*Keep hiding all the demons on the inside*
*But don't forget to paint the angel on the outside.*
*We all know*
*Don't you know*
*Who's the fool in this crowd?*

*She doesn't like the way I walk.*
*She doesn't like the words I choose.*
*Well, that's a damn shame*
*I wouldn't want it any other way.*
*I guess the world will have to end another day.*

*Everybody asks*
*But no one wants to know.*
*Take me as I am*
*Or watch me as I go.*

*Keep wanting to be welcome on the inside*
*But won't forget the ones who loved me on the outside*

*They don't like the way I dress.*
*They won't give up till the tears fall down my face.*
*But I'd never have it any other way*
*I guess the world will have to end another day.*

*They can't stand the way I get back on my feet.*
*They won't like what I've become.*
*Well, that's a damn shame*
*I wouldn't have it any other way.*
*Looks like the world will have to end another day*
*Not today . . .*

# Girl Wars

## BY CRISSA-JEAN CHAPPELL

*They circle the cafeteria in packs*
*Solid as prime numbers.*
*Girls wage war with their laser stares*
*Designer jeans in identical shades*
*Of acid wash.*
*Fake nails and bulletproof bangs*
*Trapper Keepers, hard plastic folders*
*Splattered in neon unicorns*
*Leak out whispers*
*"Insert Your Name Here."*
*Pockets swollen with crime-scene evidence*
*In Bubblicious letters*

*The note drifts around like a wheezy cough*

*You catch it.*
*Then catch on.*

*Your initials scraped into college-ruled paper*
*Furred with doodles*
*A felt-tipped mug shot*
*Flow charts of your faults*
*No telling who started it*
*Last period during AP Biology*
*Boxes checked yes/no/maybe*
*Breaking down your hair*
*Unpermed, uncut*
*Since kindergarten.*
*Your sneakers, Pez-purple high-tops*
*Your attitude, a vapor trail*
*Too skinny, too weird, too much.*
*"Maybe she'd look better*
*If she actually wore makeup, a padded bra*
*Or gained twenty pounds."*
*At the bottom, a barbed-wire suggestion*
*"She should just stop eating."*

*You can totally relate to the paramecium*
*Squirming inside that electron microscope*
*All your secret pieces*
*Magnified*

*Spend lunchtime alone in the band room*
*Drawing*
*Epic space battles*
*Under your desk.*
*Graphic novels that never get past*
*The first page.*
*Plotlines about girls with magical powers*
*Because X-ray vision is so overrated.*
*You'd rather be*
*Invisible.*

# The Curtain

## BY DEBORAH KERBEL

Me and *them*. A curtain divides us. I hide behind it, peeking out every now and then. Like a rabbit poking a nose out from its safe little hole in the ground; sniffing the air for danger.

A sharp voice shoots across the cafeteria toward my shelter. A second later, unwanted fingers slide up the spine of my still braless back. A deep, lip-curling laugh slices over my head.

I shrivel in my seat. And then comes a wet hiss so close I can feel it on my skin. A four-letter bullet grazes my ears—brands itself onto my brain like a filthy tattoo. Shivers crawl up my neck. Hunching over, I duck my face down until the curtain closes back around me like a cloak. Thin and scraggly, but it does the job. I shrink small, smaller, smallest. I shrink until I'm almost gone. Almost, but not quite. Invisibility, you see, is the unattainable dream. How easy it would be if I could glide through these halls without even making a ripple. Slide through the days, months, years of school and emerge safe and unscarred on the other side.

If only.

I wait and pray for the threat to pass. As soon as I hear the squeak of their sneakers fading away, I release the long breath I'd been clutching for comfort. My curtain sways with the force of it. I freeze until the long, dark blond strands settle back into place.


The echo of Mom's standard before-school lecture scratches at my brain. Her disappointment has become a daily routine in our house that's as predictable as burned toast.

"Why won't you cut your hair?"

*And give up my shield? Are you crazy?* I didn't ever actually say this.

She reached out a gentle hand. "It's just so long and shaggy."

I ducked out of the way, swallowed the lump of guilt rising in my throat.

"Mom, please . . ."

"It's just that we can barely see your face anymore. Don't you know how beautiful you are?"

I lowered my head. The compliment didn't make it through the curtain. It plopped at my feet like a pickled biology frog.

"I like my hair like this" is what I said. *I left out the word* need. "I'm going to grow it as long as I can and you can't stop me." *It helps me hide. Believe me, Mom, if I had what it took to grow a beard and a mustache, I probably would.*

If only.

But I didn't say this, either. Shame has bound my truth and stolen away my words. How do you tell your mother you've become a target, a loser, a failure, a lunchtime joke?

I'm pretty sure the girl I used to be is still lurking somewhere inside my head. But her voice has been crushed into a squeak, a whisper . . . a breath above silence. Funny— inside the curtain, my thoughts roar like thunderbolts. But thoughts just aren't enough to make *them* go away. And whispers are never heard. And squeaks are for mice.

The bell rings. I jump to my feet and dart out of the cafeteria, hidden behind my veil of hair, silent as a ghost. If only I could have known then what I know now (now that I've arrived safely, but not without battle scars, on the other side).

That one day soon, words won't be weapons. Instead, they'll become friends.

That one day soon, those inner thunderbolts will crash mightily overhead.

That one day soon, being different from *them* will be a gift.

That one day soon, it won't matter what *they* think.

Or say.

That one day soon, the beautiful girl hiding behind the curtain will be strong enough to step out into the light.

If only I could tell myself to just hold on until then.

*Hold on.*

REGRET

# The Eulogy of Ivy O'Conner
## BY SOPHIE JORDAN

As senior class president, it's my ~~duty~~ honor to say some words on the life of Ivy O'Conner.

Ivy attended our high school since ~~freshman~~ sophomore year, and although ~~I never spoke to her~~ we weren't the closest friends, I remember ~~everyone making fun of~~ her. How can anyone forget ~~Creepy~~ Ivy? I'll always think of her with ~~guilt~~ fondness.

Students were always ~~teasing~~ complimenting her about her ~~acne~~ eyes. She had ~~a funny mothball smell~~ a way about her, too. Everyone ~~talked about~~ noticed her. She had such a creative personality. I remember ~~her doodling stupid little shapes on her notebooks~~ she was a great artist. She loved ~~the flute~~ the clarinet music.

~~Not everyone was nice to her.~~ Not everyone understood

her. ~~Creepy~~ Ivy was so ~~strange~~ ~~different~~ unique. Whenever she was called on in class, you could count on her to say the ~~weirdest~~ most thought-provoking words. Even the teachers ~~laughed~~ looked forward to hearing her thoughts. She was ~~a freak~~ an advocate for protecting the environment. She ~~wasted~~ devoted a lot of time to that ~~crap~~ stuff.

~~Creepy~~ Ivy wasn't your average ~~nut job~~ girl walking the halls of our high school. The girl had ~~no~~ style. In my mind, I still see her in that ~~heinous~~ lovely green sweater. She was so ~~unaware when people did mean things to her~~ tolerant of others.

We might not have known what we had in her, but we will never forget her. We don't know what could have prompted her to take her life, but I wish . . .

I wish I could have stopped her. . . .

# Regret

## BY LISA YEE

I learned a lot in elementary school, like fractions, linking verbs, and that the capital of Iowa is Des Moines. From time to time, our class even performed plays. It was fun wearing a costume and pretending to be someone else. However, the real drama took place on the playground. It was a festering cesspool of innuendo and gossip. . . .

*"Sarah hates Liz."*

*"Jenny loves Tim."*

*"Andy ate his boogers again."*

Okay, so maybe it wasn't too dramatic, and the gossip was minor. Still, there was something thrilling about whispering about others, although it was miserable when you were the one being talked about or teased.

I made it through elementary school relatively unscathed

compared to what some others went through. The most torment I received had to do with my height. I was short. (I still am.) Everyone seemed to find this funny, and kids, including those who were only a millimeter taller than I, made it a point to call me names.

*Shrimp.*

*Shorty.*

*Midget.*

Putting someone down was a sport. Like dodgeball, it could be fun or scary, depending on where you stood. However, instead of balls being hurled at you, it was insults. If you were lucky, eventually the teasing would move on to someone else and you could exhale.

The entire school must have released a collective sigh of relief the day that Madge Cutler came to town. In our middle class suburb on the outskirts of Los Angeles, we didn't get many new kids. Like all my friends, my family had two cars and we lived in a tract home that was within earshot of our neighbors. Except for the slightly varying colors of paint from the same tasteful palette, every fourth house looked just like the other.

Soon enough word spread that the new girl lived in an apartment near the shopping center. Madge was too tall, boney, and the palest person I had ever seen. Her hair was stringy and the color of dust, and she kept it in a ponytail, which only served to accentuate her gaunt face. However, it was more than looks that set Madge apart. Maybe it was the way she hunched over, or the fact that she wore the same brown plaid dress with a frayed collar almost every day. Then there was the matter of her name. My classmates answered to the likes of Linda and Susan and Sandy. "Madge" sounded like a name that belonged to someone's aunt.

I'm not sure when it started or who started it. Before Madge arrived, all the teasing had been buckshot. Making fun of someone here and there. It didn't last long, and it wasn't too mean, and it certainly wasn't organized. However, when Madge appeared on the scene it was as if she wore a giant target on her chest and everyone took aim. No one ever physically hit her—we were too civilized for that. Instead we used our words.

There was something about her that empowered even the quiet kids to say mean things. Perhaps Madge's crime was that she was different. She was poor and acted the part. One afternoon I was with friends at Thrifty's drugstore getting a pistachio ice cream cone when we spotted Madge and her brother. They were dragging big stuffed pillowcases. Behind them was a woman who looked tired. It took us a while to figure out that they were going to the Laundromat. If Madge saw us, she didn't say anything. However, we dutifully told everyone that we saw her.

Then there was the time when a bunch of kids were playing on the monkey bars. When it was Madge's turn, her dress blew up. If this happened to any of the other girls, it would be no big deal. We knew enough to wear shorts under our dresses, but apparently no one had informed Madge about the dress code. There was a stunned silence. Then, all at once, everyone broke out laughing so loud that it rang across the playground. Not only was she not wearing shorts but her underwear was worn *over* her tights. That gave us enough ammunition to last for a week.

On another day, Madge walked into the classroom with her bangs newly shorn. They were too short and uneven, like she had cut them herself. When Curt Wetzel shouted, "What happened, did the gardener mistake you for a weed?" we all roared. Forget sitcoms. We had Madge to keep us amused. In my autograph book Darren Lee wrote: *May the smell of Madge Cutler linger up your nose.*

It's been decades since I last saw Madge. From time to time I've googled her, in hopes of finding out that she has become rich and famous or, at least, happy. While I never called her names to her face, what I did was just as bad, or worse. Why?

Because I passed along the gossip.

Because when people teased her, I did nothing to stop it.

Because when the crowd laughed at her, I did, too.

Funny what we remember, isn't it? Or rather, what we can't forget.

After all these years, I can't forget Madge Cutler, though I am certain she'd want to forget all of us.

# Karen

## BY NANCY WERLIN

In my sophomore year of high school, I had a smart, strong-willed friend named Karen. I've been thinking about Karen lately because her younger sister, Melanie, recently friended me on Facebook. Once I figured out why Melanie's name was familiar, I asked her how Karen was.

"Karen died a few years ago," Melanie replied. "I'm so glad we have her beautiful children."

That was all she said. And even though this was only a Facebook message, I could almost feel in its tone that Melanie had the same kind of fierceness that Karen did. I didn't push her for details, as I didn't wish to intrude or cause her pain. Melanie wanted to ask me about my books, and so we talked about that. But I was reeling. Karen died in her early forties? How could that be?

In my mind, I see Karen as she was at fifteen. She was very beautiful, with high cheekbones, huge brown eyes, and a large nose. She also had the kind of blond hair that everyone dreams of. Karen's hair hung, long and thick and golden, all the way to her waist. If you saw Karen from behind, her hair brushed and flowing, you might think she was a Barbie doll kind of girl. But then she'd turn. I think it was her nose that saved Karen from looking like Barbie; her nose that made her beautiful rather than pretty. That nose told you that this was a girl with character.

Our group of friends wasn't among the popular; we were a socially middling group mostly known for getting good grades. Boys were of interest, but we were still shy and awkward. Karen, too. At first.

But as in a contemporary YA novel, Karen the beautiful caught the eye of the most handsome and popular boy in our grade. His name was Danny. I'd never put a character like Danny in a novel because he seemed like a walking cliché: tall, dark, broad-shouldered, handsome. Of course he played football.

Danny liked Karen. Karen liked Danny. But then came the inevitable complication: Danny's previous girlfriend.

I don't remember her name. She was a year older. Weirdly (or maybe not), she looked a lot like Karen. She had a strong face that spoke of character (including, yes, a large nose). She also had hair. Her brown hair was exactly as long and as thick and as beautiful as Karen's blond hair.

This girlfriend, who was a popular cheerleader (more clichés), was furious at being replaced. And she had friends who seemed equally furious on her behalf. And so, suddenly, smart, studious, ferocious Karen was the target of a vicious bullying campaign. And Karen's allies—girls like me—were not equipped to be the kind of support that could really help her much against the older, popular girls who were after her. Karen's life became abruptly miserable.

But Karen fought back anyway. It was in her nature. Karen fought back as hard as she could.

Where was Danny in all this, you ask? Why didn't he defend his new girlfriend? Well, that's where things get even more interesting. It turned out that maybe Danny hadn't exactly broken up with the old girlfriend before getting started with Karen. It turned out that maybe Danny felt as if he was entitled to all the long-haired beauties he wanted. It turned out that maybe Danny liked being fought over . . . and did things to egg it on, favoring first one girl, and then the other. . . .

I won't dwell on the weeks in which Karen was under siege, believing that Danny cared for her, and that the enemy was this vicious, older girl who looked so much like her. And I can't tell you what was in Karen's mind, because—like her sister today—Karen kept her deepest emotions to herself. And I don't know what the other girl was thinking, either, as she fought the girl she believed to be her enemy.

But I bet there was one person having a really good time.

Here's how I wish it had gone. Here's what I now realize I would like to have seen: those two beautiful girls, side by side, blond and brown hair streaming behind them, as they turned their backs on handsome, empty, cruel Danny and walked calmly away.

# Surviving Alfalfa

## BY TERI BROWN

He stands there, a good two feet taller than you, and he seems invincible. Until you look in his eyes and they're so dark with pain that they're almost black. The scent of freshly cut hay swirls around you.

Then he asks, "Why don't you guys like me?"

Your heart thuds in your chest and you feel his hurt and confusion as if it were your own, because you know that pain. But you can't tell him the truth. You're too scared, too confused, too insecure. So you lie.

"We like you."

He knows you're lying and shakes his head. "No. No one talks to me. You all make fun of me."

You don't correct him, because to your shame, it's true. You have made fun of him. Made fun of him because that's what *she* does and you will do anything not to be in his position, because you've been there before and, may God forgive you, you don't have the courage or the fortitude to do anything else.

Now there's anger under your pain because he's holding up a mirror and it's so ugly and scary you want to run away and hide.

You give a little laugh that doesn't sound like a laugh. "No, we like you."

And you edge away.

His face changes and you take another step back, the cut alfalfa crunching beneath your feet. He moves away from the tractor and he reaches out and squeezes one of your breasts and you don't say anything, because this is your penance for lying. Then you see the tears in his eyes as he turns away and you know he's as trapped as you are—trapped by geography, trapped by age, trapped because all you want in the world is to belong.

Bigfoot crying in the field.

And you resist running the rest of the way to your best friend's house because you don't want him to know how afraid you are. Not just of him, but of her. How even at this moment you don't know if she's going to be happy to see you or if she's with one of your other friends, talking behind your back. The thought churns in your stomach and you wonder what's wrong with you. . . . You've just been manhandled and all you're worried about is whether your best friend still likes you or not.

And you wish with all your heart you lived anywhere but here, in Alfalfa, a tiny community so far away from your high school that it takes the bus forty-five minutes to get to and from school. A lot can happen in forty-five minutes. Just ask Matt. Or Michelle. Or Dina. Or Stewart. Or Bigfoot. Yeah, Bigfoot. You're pretty sure you knew his real name at one time, and it's ironic that all you remember is the name that your BFF gave him.

Bigfoot crying in the field.

When you and your BFF are friends, life is magic. Everything is more fun when she's there; long trail rides in the woods, midnight movies, and sneaking out to swim in the canals late at night.

Then it all ends.

You'll wake up one morning and for no reason you can discern, you'll be on the outside looking in. You're the one afraid to get on the bus. Afraid of the walk home. Afraid of going out riding. Afraid to answer the phone. Afraid, afraid, afraid. But avoiding them doesn't help. She and the others ride up to your house on their horses and call you out. Taunting you, threatening you.

The first time she turned on you was because you suggested having a club like in Judy Blume's *Are You There God? It's Me, Margaret.* Suddenly, you're the girl who wanted a club about periods (as she announced to the whole bus, boys and all). Humiliation was her weapon of choice, and if that didn't work, she would have someone dump perfume on the unlucky victim on her way to school. She rarely did her own dirty work.

During the BFF times, you're by her side as she intimidates others. You just go along. So does everyone else. You keep your mouth shut; you close your eyes and you pretend it's not happening. Maybe if you pretend hard enough it won't be true. But it always is and their pain and humiliation only illustrates how you do *not* want to be in their shoes again. Ever.

So you take the coward's way out. Live in fear. And wait for your turn at the whipping post.

Bigfoot crying in the field.

Now, as an adult, you wish you could go back and change it all. You see yourself strong, as strong as you are now. You see yourself standing up for Matt and Dina and Michelle and Stewart. And Bigfoot. Especially Bigfoot. You want to wipe away the tears and the confusion and the hurt of that sixteen-year-old boy. And you want to tell him you're sorry. Sorry that you left him there, crying in the field.

But you can't change anything and the memory of leaving that man/child broken by the tractor will hurt you forever. But you survived. And all you can do is share your strength with others, with teens who have been bullied or who are afraid to do anything about those who bully. And you try and you try and you hope that you're helping, but behind it all you can still see him.

Bigfoot crying in the field.

# When I Was a Bully, Too

## BY MELISSA WALKER

When I was in seventh grade, I was nervous all the time. Every day that I went into school to meet my friends in the hallway, I wondered if this was a day that they'd turn on me, a day when I'd get teased and made fun of. Or if it was someone else's day to take the hit.

There was one girl in our tight-knit group of four, Eliza[*], who led the charge—always. It would start with a little comment: "Nice shirt, Mel." And then Leigh and Ariel would join in—"Yeah, nice shirt. Did you get that at the thrift shop?" It didn't matter if I'd spent an hour trying to figure out what to wear that wouldn't attract attention, that would fit in, that would keep them from singling me out.

I have to admit that I was relieved when it wasn't me

---

[*] All names have been changed because these girls? They'll totally recognize themselves.

who got picked on. Leigh and Ariel took the brunt of Eliza's seemingly random insults, too. There was no way to deflect them—we all ganged up on whoever was chosen for sacrifice that day.

Until one night, when Eliza was home sick and Leigh, Ariel, and I went to a junior high dance together. We gathered in the corner of the gym, and Leigh said, "Eliza's kind of pissing me off lately." She said it tentatively, like she wasn't sure if we'd agree. But both Ariel and I nodded and smiled. That night, the three of us formulated a plan.

The plan wasn't complicated, it wasn't nuanced, it had very few steps. The plan was: Let's stop talking to Eliza. Just ignore her. Do that thing where you say, "Do you hear a fly buzzing around?" whenever she talks.

And we did. We shut her out in the hallway before the morning bell, we turned our backs to her at lunch, we didn't wait for her between classes. It was brutal.

When she cornered me alone at my locker and demanded to know what was going on, I ignored her, as I'd pledged to Ariel and Leigh that I'd do. I walked down the hallway quickly as Eliza followed me, and I heard her start to cry.

Eliza and I used to talk every day on the phone after school. But when she called that day, sobbing and wanting to know what she'd done, I hung up on her.

After that she left us alone. It took one day to end what felt like a lifetime of tyranny (really, it was about a year). But it left me feeling empty, cold, like I didn't have a circle of friends anymore.

I stayed friends with Ariel and Leigh, but we all went into our separate groups in high school. Eliza and I said "Hi" in the halls, but we were never close again.

This summer, a mutual friend of mine and Eliza's commented on a photo Eliza had posted on Facebook, so it showed up in my feed. I clicked through to see a little girl with Eliza's smile, maybe two years old—her daughter.

I remembered playing Nintendo at Eliza's house, making up hilarious dances in her living room, filming a movie in sixth grade where we dressed up in her mom's clothes and delivered soap opera–quality lines. I remembered how she could say and do things that would make me giggle until I'd end up lying on the ground, doubled over in laughter.

And here is what I wished: I wished that Eliza had been kinder, yes, not such a bully. But I also wish that Ariel and Leigh and I had made a different plan that night. One where we told Eliza that she was mean a lot of the time, made it clear to her that we wouldn't gang up on one another for entertainment. And then, the next time she said something barbed like, "Nice shirt, Mel," Ariel and Leigh would have said, "It is nice. Where'd you get it?" and the situation would have been diffused.

The problem was that we were all too scared to be the one who stood up for the first time. So we avoided Eliza's wrath by shutting her out completely.

Bullies have foot soldiers. And those people can turn into bullies themselves, like we did against Eliza. But they don't have to. They can make better, if harder, choices. And I wish I had.

# Carol

## BY AMY GOLDMAN KOSS

I held power briefly in sixth grade. I didn't hold ultimate, unquestionable power, and I didn't rule alone, but still, my power was nothing to scoff at. One of the perks of being in the ruling class at Greenfield Elementary was that I had a Carol.

Here's where I'd tell you about Carol if I knew anything, but I didn't know where she lived or if she had brothers or sisters or any of that. I knew only that if I got right up in her face and accused her of terrible things, and said mean, horrible things about her, every part of her froze—except for her eyes. Her eyes got wide and panicky and darted around as if she was looking for an escape. But she didn't escape, she just stood there until I was done and released her. I imagine it didn't make Carol feel so great, but it made me feel terrific!

I can't tell you why I picked Carol because I don't know. Maybe I was like a hungry lion chasing the herd of elk, looking for the easiest one to separate and take down. Or maybe it was because she was unprotected. I assume that if she hadn't been alone I would have chosen someone who was. I was a bully but not quite powerful enough to take on more than one victim. Maybe Carol hadn't been alone to start with, but whatever friends she'd had abandoned her in fear and self-preservation when they saw that she had been selected as my prey.

I knew that what I was doing was beyond bad. My family would be absolutely horrified if they knew. Horrified and shocked. Actually, I was horrified myself, but that added to the rush. It was thrilling to be so bad. It made my whole body practically vibrate with life and power. And after a few minutes of tormenting Carol, I felt a sort of peace as my heart calmed back down and the sweat on my hands tingled and evaporated.

Tormenting Carol was like a gateway drug to the thrill of being bad. The next year I learned to smoke cigarettes and weed. Soon after that I was popping whatever kind of pill anyone offered. But that's a different story.

A few months deeper into sixth grade, there was a power shift, and I myself was divided from the herd. I was outraged but not surprised. Such was the nature of sixth grade. I remember toying with the idea of teaming up with Carol, forming a little band of outcasts, but when I sidled up to her on the playground, she held her hand up like a stop sign and said, "Don't even bother to try!"

# Never Shut Up

## BY KIERSTEN WHITE

It was the middle of Government and Politics class, and though the teacher was lecturing, the boy sitting behind me hadn't gotten off the previous topic. He shrugged, whispering, "I don't think that sexism and racism are problems in our country anymore. People just pretend they are."

My face turned red and I jabbed a single accusatory finger at him. "*White male*, you have no perspective!"

It was loud.

Oh, so loud.

I was always inadvertently entertaining in that class. Everyone knew that if you brought up one of my pet topics, I was good for an impassioned debate. Senior year my class awarded the yearbook spots. Alongside "Most Likely to Succeed" and "Best Smile" was my award: "Always Has Something to Say." But when they put it under my picture, they changed the title to "Never Shuts Up." Because I never. Shut. Up.

Problem is, for all my not shutting up, I never managed to *speak* up. In the end, how much did the glass ceiling impact my working two shifts a week at the local sandwich shop? How much did gun control issues factor into my daily life? What good was all of my passion and crusading and adopting of causes doing *any* of the people around me every day?

I liked having causes and caring about things, but only if they were safe. I could talk for days about feminism because it didn't impact me, didn't threaten me, didn't put me in an uncomfortable position. Safe.

But that day I saw those kids teasing a special ed student in the hallway, making him sing louder and louder while they laughed at his innocent enthusiasm? I didn't say anything. I knew those kids. We weren't friends, exactly, but we weren't not friends. And while what they were doing made me sick to my stomach, saying something felt too dangerous. What if I said something and they decided to be cruel to me instead? And what about the boy? He thought they were his friends, couldn't understand what they were doing. I wasn't going to explain it to him. It was too complicated, too hard, too involved.

So I did the easy thing. I walked away. And I've always regretted it. I wonder now how much of an impact I could have made if I'd really always had something to say. If I'd said the things that mattered, stood up for people who actually needed my help, gotten involved instead of keeping my head down.

In this era of visibility, where everyone can see what anyone says about anything on social networking sites, it's even more obvious to see kids being hurt, being bullied, being the victims of cruelty. I wonder if I'd had that access as a teen, would I have been the one to call out bullies and tell them to shut up? Would I have stood up for the people too exhausted by ceaseless torment to stand up for themselves?

Would I finally have decided to really have something to say?

I don't know. I hope so. Because being a bully is easy, and being a victim is all too common. But standing on your safe middle ground and deciding to reach out where you can make a difference? That is a rare and difficult choice.

Make the choice. Do something. *Never* shut up.

I wish I had.

# The Day I Followed
## BY ERIC LUPER

"Only one last test and you're in the club," I said to Sam, who was trotting alongside me like a puppy eager for a treat. I could feel excitement radiate off him as we walked to the far side of Henshaw Park.

Sam fiddled with the zipper of his hoodie. "What do I have to do?" he asked.

"It's easy," I said, not quite sure what I had in store for him.

Ricky Parillo had told Sam that there was a series of tests you had to pass in order to get in with the group of kids who hung out at the park, and Sam had been begging all afternoon. The least we could do was give him something to do.

I glanced back at the bench near the swings. The other neighborhood kids—Ricky; Mark; the twins, Glen and

Gary; and a few guys I didn't know—urged me on with grins and fist pumps. It had been only a few days since Ricky had pegged me in the back of the head with a basketball and I figured I'd rather be on the dealing side of things for a change. Anyhow, Sam could take it. He'd been putting up with this sort of stuff long before I moved to town.

At least that's what I'd heard.

It started off simple: sprint a few laps around the park, go buy us gum at the candy store, hang upside down from the monkey bars for five minutes, anything we could think of to amuse ourselves.

On all counts, Sam eagerly did what we told him to do.

And on all counts I was glad it wasn't me.

"The last test is on the tennis courts," I said.

"You sure every one of you had to do all these things?" Sam asked skeptically.

"Of course," I lied. I unlatched the heavy gate and led Sam to the net.

My mind scrambled to think of something that would give the other kids a good laugh. "I'm going to blindfold you and you have to find your way out."

I figured watching Sam bumble around on the green concrete would be pretty funny. Maybe he'd even trip over the net.

"That's lame," he said.

"I told you it was easy."

Sam smiled. His crooked teeth spread his lips apart. His

wavy hair stuck to his forehead in sweaty swirls. He was such an easy target, so odd-looking, so gullible. It was no wonder most of the fifth graders picked on the kid.

I felt a pang of guilt.

But it was only a pang.

The rest of me felt relieved it wasn't me going through this fake initiation.

"What are you going to blindfold me with?" Sam asked.

"I don't know." I patted my pockets. "Do you have anything?"

"I could put my hoodie on backward," he offered. "You know, so the hood covers my face."

"Great idea."

Sam pulled his arms out of the sleeves and turned his sweatshirt around. Then he flipped his hood up over his face. "I'm totally blind!" he joked as he flailed his arms around dramatically. I could hear the smile in his voice.

The other guys cheered from across the park.

Something fluttered in my chest. Was it fear? Excitement? Maybe it was something else. What I knew was that it was the first time I'd felt in control in a while. I had been struggling for friends ever since I moved here in third grade. Amusing the kids at the park, getting on their good side, seemed an excellent way to do it.

"All right," I said. "I'll just turn you around a few times . . ."

Sam held out his arms so I could spin him more easily.

I glanced at the other kids. Ricky gave me a thumbs-up.

When I figured Sam was dizzy enough, I let him go. He spun around a few extra times for good measure. By the time I slipped out of the tennis court, Sam was staggering about, groping for anything to help him regain his bearings. He stumbled to the edge of the court and leaned a shoulder against the fence. For a moment I was both afraid and amused that he might throw up inside his own hood.

*Probably just playing it up to make us laugh,* I thought.

That's when Mark pushed past me onto the court and held Sam against the fence. Ricky pulled the strings of Sam's hoodie through the bars and yanked them tight so Sam's head was snug against the metal. Then he tied a triple knot. Sam cried out but Mark and Ricky dashed away. I looked for Glen and Gary, but the twins were already gone, having hoisted Sam's new ten-speed high into the branches of a nearby tree. Everyone else was running, too.

"Let's go!" someone called to me.

I watched Sam struggle to loosen the drawstrings of his sweatshirt. His skinny legs kicked at the air. His fingers clawed at the back of his head.

"Someone untie me!" he shouted between sobs. "I can't reach the knot through the fence!"

I hesitated. Even with my short nails, I knew I could get the knot loose.

I heard the laughter fade toward Ricky's house.

"Come on, Luper!" someone else yelled. "Follow us!"

I followed.

The cracked sidewalk passed easily under my feet. I knew the way to Ricky's. It was backed up to the train tracks on Hawthorne Avenue. I passed it every day on my way home from school, saw them eating ice pops on the front stoop out of the corner of my eye. I never dared to look up after the one time Mark chucked his blue raspberry Freezee at me.

*Maybe we'll have ice pops when we get there. Maybe those guys will let me hang out with them on the front stoop.*

A heavy lump rose in my chest.

I slowed.

*Maybe they won't pick on me anymore . . .*

I stopped.

I heard Sam's muffled cries behind me.

I turned around . . .

. . . and headed back to the park.

Even with my short nails, I knew I could get the knot loose.

THANK YOU, FRIENDS

# The Alphabet

## BY LAURA KASISCHKE

**A.** I blamed the alphabet that the last name of the boy who hated me started with a letter so close to the letter that started mine. The ruthless fact of that. The depth and relentlessness of his random-seeming hatred. And he would be sitting right behind me in seventh-grade homeroom for the rest of my life. It made me want to die.

**B.** "Because he's jealous of you?" my mother offered (so kind, so wrong) when I asked what could possibly have made this boy hate me so, so much. "Maybe you have something he wishes he had?"

**C.** Could my mother not see that I was no one a boy like this would be jealous of? My hair. My skin. My clothes. The house we lived in. The car my father drove.

**D.** "Don't raise your hand," he whispered into my neck as I was just about to answer a question.

**E.** "Everybody hates your goody-goody 'I know the answer, I know the answer.'"

**F.** Forgotten, over the years, until I remember it for you: The emptiness inside me every morning as I sat down at that desk. If he was already in his seat, I had to endure whatever he would say that day about my hair, my skin, my clothes, the house we lived in, the car my father drove. If he wasn't there yet, I would keep my eyes on the book in front of me and wait. Some mornings, a mist of spit (he was so good at this, keeping anyone from seeing it) from above me. Some mornings, nothing, which meant—

**G.** "Get ready."

**H.** The hallway. There, the teachers would see nothing.

**I.** I hurried. To the next class. To my locker. To the bathroom. But when I stepped out, there he was. He liked to kick the books out of my arms. An explosion of them around me, and me on the floor. Me, trying to gather them back up as he kicked them out of reach.

**J.** Jar. It was for science. We'd had to catch moths and grasshoppers and whatever else we could, bring them to class in a glass jar with holes poked in the lid. I had that jar in my hands and was hurrying, almost there, and then he was also there, and the jar was smashing on the floor around me. The billion pieces of that, and the living creatures fluttering, hopping, crawling, some escaping, some dying.

**K.** The first letter of my last name.

**L.** The first letter of his last name.

**M.** My mother pointed out an article in the newspaper about this boy's sister. She had been paralyzed in a car accident the year before. A lawsuit. A photograph of this girl in a wheelchair. Her sad expression. Her twisted hands in her lap. This boy's house behind her. It was a mansion, but all the curtains were pulled closed.

**N.** No one noticed who it was who might have torn my homework in half that morning and thrown it on the floor when I'd gotten up to go to the office. They'd called me down to pick up my homework from the day before, which had disappeared and been found wadded up in a trash can.

**O.** "Oh, maybe he likes you. Maybe he's trying to get your attention."

**P.** "Piss," he said. "Why do you always stink like piss? Is it because you live in that shitty little house?" At home, I smelled all my clothes, my underarms. I asked my mother to smell my hair. I bought soap and shampoo and feminine hygiene products. He never said it again, but I walked through the world smelling myself smelling like piss. I tried not to stand too close to the boy I liked. My best friend smelled me every day and insisted (such a good friend) that I smelled like violets.

**Q.** "Quit paying so much attention, and he'll quit picking on you," said the one teacher I ever told. "Fuck her," my best friend said when I relayed this information. "How do you not pay attention when someone kicks the books out of your hands?" We laughed long and hard about that. We acted out the scenario: Me, walking happily through the hallways with an armload of books, whistling a tune. Him, stomping toward me, the little two-step run-and-kick he had perfected, and the books in the air while I just stood there pretending nothing had happened. The books landed on my head, and I stood there, smiling, and said, "Hi, Tom! How are you this morning?"

**R.** "Rat head," he called me, and stuck a wad of gum in my hair.

**S.** She was the first person I thought to call, to tell. Thirty-five years later, separated now by hundreds of miles, living in a world we could never have imagined. Husbands, children, pets, houses, neighbors who liked us, colleagues who listened to our opinions politely. Whole decades had passed in this world, the real one, in which people were either kind or, at worst, indifferent. When I sat down in a chair, I never considered who might be sitting behind me. For more than a quarter of a century I had not once cringed and looked behind me, and had I really even thought of him in all that time?

Maybe a little. Maybe I told the story to entertain my husband or one of the kids. A story of this awful boy who kicked a jar of grasshoppers out of my hands. Who stuck a wad of gum in my hair. I'd tell it, and it was funny. Even to me. These things had happened to another girl—one so afraid of a boy in her homeroom that she went home every day and smelled her clothes. Who assumed she always would. Who believed that seventh-grade homeroom would last forever. Who blamed the unchangeable alphabet—cold and distant and as out of her control as the cosmos.

Over. That other forever was over and had only been called up again that afternoon in front of the computer when his much-older face emerged from the void in which I'd left it—with an invitation. To be friends. (The internet: it hadn't been invented yet, or what an added tool it would have been, back then, for him to torture me with!) I thought, briefly, I should be upset, but found myself laughing instead and dialing the number of my old friend.

"Who? Tell me."

T. "Tom L."

U. "Unbelievable. What did you do?" "Nothing." "What will you do?" "I'm still thinking about that." "Maybe he's going to apologize. Or maybe he's not done bullying you yet." "Oh, yes he is," I said.

V. "Life is very strange," she said. "Very, very strange. Who would ever have imagined?"

W. "Why me?" I asked, as if there might be an answer to that question after all this time. We laughed.

X. "Exactly," she said.

Y. "You can't take it personally," my mother said, wiping the tears off my cheeks, my chin, my neck with her soft hand. (But I wanted to die. But I wanted to die. I remember so little, but I remember clearly: Because of him, I wanted to die.) "If you weren't there to bully, it would just be someone else. You're going to be stronger and happier after you live through this, I promise you."

2. How could she have been so wrong? (So wrong. So kind.) How could she have been so right? All the years and friends and family and the sorrows and the strength I would need and the laughter. On the other side of that forever was the future, and it was so much better, and all I needed to do was to keep on living to get to it.

# They Made Me Do It and I'm Sorry

BY CECIL CASTELLUCCI

ILLUSTRATED BY LISE BERNIER

168

AND THEN AFTER A WEEK OR TWO, IT WAS SOMEONE ELSE'S TURN FOR THE SILENT TREATMENT.

NO ONE EVER TALKED ABOUT HOW TERRIBLE IT WAS.

AND NO ONE EVER STOOD UP TO THE GROUP.

173

THEY MADE ME DO IT AND I'M SORRY!

THIS IS WHAT I SAID...

THE SILENT TREATMENT IS DUMB.

I KNOW. IT TOTALLY IS.

I WONDERED WHAT WOULD HAPPEN THE NEXT DAY AT SCHOOL.

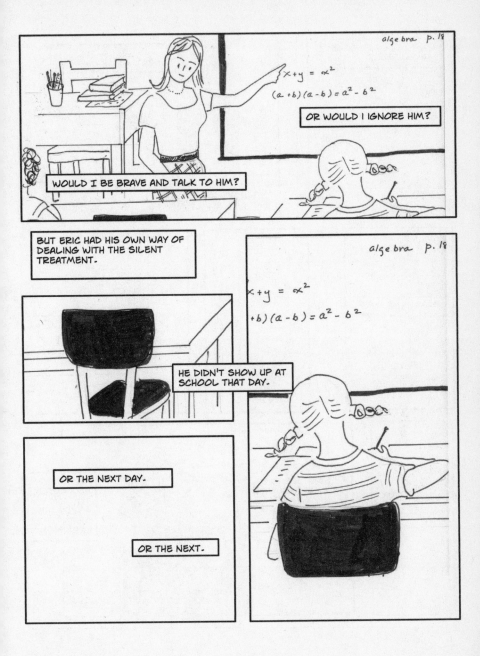

WHEN ERIC CAME BACK TO SCHOOL, EVERYONE ACTED LIKE NOTHING HAD HAPPENED.

BUT I WAS WORRIED.

RELAX. IT'S OVER.

I KNEW IT WAS JUST A MATTER OF TIME BEFORE SOMEONE WAS IGNORED AGAIN.

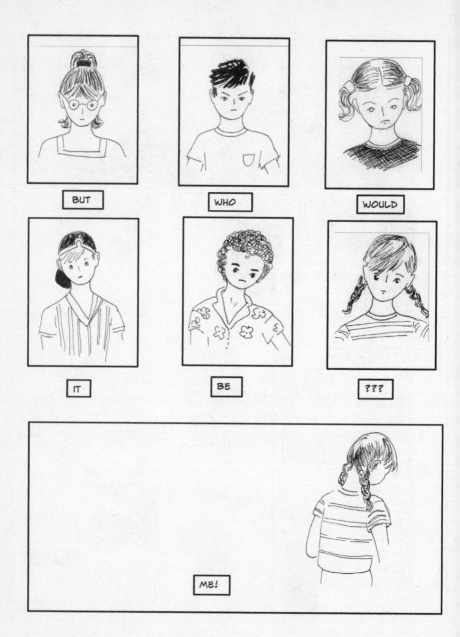

179

# Simplehero

## BY DEBBIE RIGAUD

I'm not what you would call a tough girl. In fact, I'd say I'm more of the scaredy-cat persuasion. I've never been in a school-yard fight. I was always of the opinion that someone as bony as I should avoid physical confrontation. So imagine my confusion when my friend Desiree told me that I protected her from a notoriously fearsome bully our freshman year in high school.

"You don't remember?" she asked me during a recent phone conversation. "That's how we became friends!"

Me? Defend Desiree? Desiree is one of the boldest people I know. Smart and opinionated, the girl can debate any attorney, seasoned politician, or TV judge to the ground. And with a flash of her dimples and a quick turn of phrase, she'll yank you out of your proverbial box and introduce you to a fresh perspective. But that's the Desiree from the later high school years and beyond. As she tells it, she was in a very different place at the start of freshman year.

"Tanya* wanted to fight me, so she made up this story that I was talking about her brother on the bus," recounts Desiree. "I was terrified—Tanya was huge, and I'm not a fighter. You and Rhonda were there, and you said, 'She didn't say that. I was on the bus and I know that's not true. She doesn't even catch the bus!'"

The story started to sound vaguely familiar to me, but it wasn't crystal clear until Desiree uttered Rhonda's now legendary words: "You'll have to get through me to get to her." That's when I got a visual on the day. We were in the school's lower level in the hallway by the lockers. As she charged toward Desiree, Tanya looked ten feet tall. She was wild-eyed with flaring nostrils, and her husky voice blared a loud and angry alarm. I remember thinking, Tanya's got the story all wrong. So I told her the truth. But Rhonda's style of defense was on a whole 'nother level. Rhonda matched Tanya in size, so she stepped between Tanya and Desiree and said, "I will not let you touch this girl. You'll have to go through me to get to her." That quelled everything outright. Tanya backed down and walked away.

I knew Des had run-ins with bullies her freshman year

---

* All names except Desiree's have been changed.

at our all-girls academy. But I never understood why. Des was as unlikely a target as I was a bodyguard. She is a tall, attractive girl from a prominent family in her suburban town. She has five older brothers—one of whom was an NFL player at the time. But as Desiree explains it, two things made her a target throughout her childhood—her dark skin and her Caribbean heritage.

In grammar and middle schools, she was called every derogatory name for "black" by lighter-skinned African-American classmates. The catchy commercial jingle lulling TV viewers to "Come Back to Jamaica" became "Go Back to Jamaica." And each year she dreaded the public reading of her classmates' annual "hot list" of girls (ranked by the boys) and boys (ranked by girls). Desiree was always at or near the bottom of that list. "I wanted to quit school even back then," she recalls.

Things changed in high school—but only slightly. Thanks to the rise of Afrocentric lyrics in rap songs, being dark-skinned became acceptable, and even cool. Yet Desiree was still singled out by bullies because of where she was from. Unlike most of the handful of African-American students who came from urban towns, Desiree lived in an affluent suburb. And while most of the black students rode the city bus to school, Desiree was driven. She missed out on all the critical bonding time on the hour-plus commute to school. (Looking back at these "commuter" and "urban dweller" categories, it seemed that—if you were black—you were all right if you fell under at least one of the categories. I fit under both categories. My close friend Cara was from the suburbs, but she caught the bus. And oddly enough, Desiree's tormentor Tanya didn't catch the bus. But she was from the city. Des, on the other hand, was 0 for 2.)

And it didn't help matters when other kids jumped on the bullies' bandwagon, joining in the chorus of insults against her. The girls Desiree thought were her friends reported to the bullies that Desiree's mother has an accent and isn't American. This led to even more taunting. "They really stuck on the 'ugly' thing for a while," she remembers. (Even though my parents are also immigrants, Des believes I was spared for having had older sisters and a cousin at the school.)

Midway through freshman year, Tanya and her sidekick—yes, she had one—became rabid in their pursuit of Desiree. Almost daily, they threatened to jump her, snatched away her lunch, and even took her jewelry—right off her hands! Tanya and Tara (the sidekick) had the habit of wearing each other's jewelry. For some reason, they felt Desiree should share in their friendship ritual.

"One day Tanya walked up to me and said, 'I wanna hold your jewelry; I wanna wear that ring,'" recounts Desiree. "The ring was on my index finger and I said, 'No, you can't; my brother gave me this ring.'" As soon as the words were out of her mouth, Tanya and Tara stepped closer, boxing Desiree in at her locker. Then Tanya grabbed her hand and pulled the ring off her finger. "I asked, 'Are you gonna give it back at the end of the day?' She said 'Yeah,' but I never got it back and she never wore it at school."

Desiree was at her breaking point. Fearing the backlash she thought would follow if she told teachers or her parents, she suffered in silence. "I had no self-worth, self-image, none of that." Then sadly, Des got so low, she attempted to take her life. "I took pills, but nothing happened. I just got sleepy. Nobody knew."

Not long after this attempt, Tanya charged Desiree in the school hallway, accusing her of trashing Tanya's brother on the bus. But before she could touch Desiree, Rhonda and I intervened.

"At the time, I had no friends," Des tells me. "But seeing the two of you stick up for me made me realize that there are kind people out there who will stick up for you regardless. It was like, I can make friends. I am worth something because somebody stuck up for me. What you and Rhonda did— that kind of saved my life."

As karma would have it, Tanya got pregnant later that year and dropped out of school. Tara moved away and didn't return after freshman year. The bullies' bandwagon disbanded and all Desiree bashing came to an end. Over the next three years, high school became a supportive, encouraging environment for Des, and she blossomed into the woman I still know and love today.

To think, a selfless act of little consequence to me, a moment I barely thought twice of again, a simple decision to get involved, changed another person's outlook on life.

And did I mention that I lean toward the scaredy-cat persuasion?

# Isolation

## BY CYNTHIA LEITICH SMITH

Let's talk about isolation.

The girl who bullied me took away two of my best friends—one, then another.

She gave them a choice, and they bought their freedom at my expense.

I was an only child, and I couldn't talk to my parents about it. It was so important to them that I be happy. I didn't dare suggest otherwise.

At school, standing beside me would've meant moving into the target zone.

For most people, that wasn't a choice they were willing to make. I didn't blame them. And I didn't want to go through that pain again, either.

So I quietly carved out some territory for myself—at

dance class, the library, the school newspaper. But that didn't make sitting alone at lunch or surviving girls' gym any easier.

I still looked over my shoulder as I walked home.

I still fretted my garage-sale and discount-store clothes.

And I still guarded the secret of my mixed-blood Native American heritage.

Then one day I noticed a girl who was even quieter than me—a fair, whip-smart girl with a strong sense of justice. Who'd had her share of run-ins with the same bully.

This time I decided to stand beside her.

*Cynthia and Tracy, the quieter girl, became friends. Years later they shared a college dorm room.*

*Cynthia went on to study law and journalism and is an author. Tracy went on to study political science and owns her own lobbying firm. Neither is especially quiet anymore.*

# Luz

## BY MELODYE SHORE

I lean against the outside wall of the cafeteria, gasping for air. Blood oozes from the long, crimson gashes on my arms, staining the stucco as it drips into the spreading pool of vomit at my feet. My stomach heaves yet again, and when there's nothing left but bile, I fix my gaze on the sliver of sunshine peeking through the clouds. *Don't cry*, I tell myself. *Don't let anyone see you cry.*

Quick footfalls echo across the courtyard. I shade my eyes and find myself staring at the brown-eyed girl who transferred into eighth-grade English not long after me. Her name is Luz, if I remember correctly, though names don't seem to matter when you're stuck in the back of an overcrowded classroom—the row reserved for misfits and newcomers.

"*Dáme tus manos.*" Her voice is gentle, her face etched with worry.

I manage a weak smile. "I'm fine," I say. "I just need a little fresh air."

Truth is, I am *not* fine. A headache throbs at my temples. When I rake my fingers through my knotted hair, I pull away clots of blood. The wounds on my arms hurt like hell. Each jagged breath is more painful than the last—never mind the soul-scorching insults still ringing in my ears.

It all started in the cafeteria bathroom. I was searching for the free meal ticket that had fallen through a hole in my pocket. The room was quiet except for the locked stall on the end, where another eighth grader was purging her lunch.

The toilet flushed. She emerged from the stall, wiping her mouth with the back of her hand.

I was startled. I tried to hide the apple in my hand— the perfectly good apple I'd retrieved from the trash can when I thought no one was looking. I wasn't sure if she'd seen me . . . until, that is, she cleared her throat.

We stared at each other's reflection, eyes mirroring our darkest secrets.

Her lips curled into a sneer. "Just wait till everyone hears about this!" she said, and then she rushed out the door.

I pulled a wad of paper towels from the dispenser, but

before I could bury the offending fruit, she returned with a posse of her friends.

"Trash picker!" someone said with a snicker.

And from someplace behind me, "Freeloader!" And worse.

I was caught off guard by their angry eyes, paralyzed by their venomous words.

They swarmed around me, mocking my silence. Then someone grabbed me from behind.

I called for help.

A fist landed in my stomach.

I wheezed, begged for mercy.

They kicked and punched me instead.

I broke free somehow and ran for the exit, but not before they yanked out handfuls of hair and shredded my arms with their fingernails.

"That's right," someone shrieked. "Go home to the Dumpster you came from!"

And now, I'm vomiting up every last bit of that apple—and with it, every last ounce of my dignity.

"Let me help you," Luz says in broken English. When she reaches for me, her outstretched arms are like wings, lifting me above and beyond all the pain and humiliation. I slip my hands into hers, and she squeezes them gently. I feel stronger already.

Hand in hand, we walk toward the main office to see the nurse. We duck underneath a sprawling eucalyptus tree, and she steadies me when I stumble over the roots. I retie my hand-me-down shoes, two sizes too large, and then we step inside.

The principal winces when we approach the counter, no doubt taking inventory of my injuries. "Who did this to you?" he asks. I don't answer for fear of retaliation.

He turns to Luz. "You must have played some part in this!" She blinks and shrugs, as if she doesn't understand him. Exasperated, he suspends us for the rest of the day.

I don't have a key to my apartment, so my new friend invites me to hers. The steamy smells of chicken and corn tortillas greet us at the door. Luz's mother is stirring a boiling pot in the kitchen, but when she sees my wounds, her spoon clatters to the linoleum floor.

Luz brings me bandages and a warm wash cloth, and in halting English, her mother insists that I stay for dinner. Her father says the blessing, and then we pile our plates high with *arroz con pollo* and *frijoles*—foods I learned to pronounce in Conversational Spanish but haven't eaten before. They smile when I ask for seconds.

We talk about our families, and Luz translates for everyone. Her father says they immigrated to California from a small village in Mexico, sneaking across the border in the dead of night. Now he follows the crops. Her mother speaks with sorrow about the relatives she can't risk seeing again, and when I discuss my parents' separation, she dabs her eyes with her apron.

By this time, our bellies are full, and the moon shines bright in the inky night sky. Tears turn to laughter, and I don't know if I'll ever be able to translate into words the sense of belonging I feel in this moment.

It's the first of many meals Luz and I eventually share, the first day of a friendship I want to last forever. We're walking home from school together when I ask, "Will we always be friends?" She looks away, and in that instant, we both know the answer.

Winter turns to spring, and when one day she disappears, I am sad but not surprised. Her desk sits unoccupied for days, but no one questions her absence. I call her, but the phone's been disconnected. I knock, and then ring her doorbell, but the curtains stand open and the apartment is vacant.

I think back to the day she came to my rescue. Luz, whose name means light . . . Luz, my beacon of hope in the darkness. Tears stream down my face unchecked, and I don't care if anyone sees me cry.

# Dear Caroline from Canada
## BY CARRIE RYAN

Dear Caroline from Canada,

I know we last saw each other on the Western Tour in the summer of 1993 and you've probably forgotten me. But I'm not sure I ever really thanked you. I'm not sure I even understood how brave you were until I got older.

Just in case you don't remember . . . We were at the dude ranch in Wyoming and some girl (I can't remember her name but I'll call her Ginger) said she wanted a cowboy. The only cowboy at the ranch our age asked *me* to dance (he even sang "Wonderful Tonight" in my ear—I still love that song) and that ticked her off, so she told him, and everyone else, that I was gay.

Today I'd just laugh at her. I'm embarrassed that being called gay was even an insult back then. And it's not really that that insulted me; it's that we had to share rooms and beds with other girls on the tour and suddenly they all gave me the evil eye when we were paired up. We weren't allowed to walk around unless we were in groups of three and no one—*no one*—would let me hang out with them.

I had to beg to tag along behind random groups so I wouldn't get in trouble.

It was in the mall after the bus broke down when you told me what Ginger said—until then I had no idea why everyone suddenly hated me that much. All I knew was that I was ostracized—utterly and completely cast out.

So alone. Humiliated.

But you paired up with me that day. You told me the truth even though it was difficult and you promised that you'd be my friend and never leave me out again.

I was so selfish I was just glad to have a friend. I didn't think about what that meant for you and your reputation. Suddenly everyone called you my gay girlfriend and you were cast out just as much as I was.

It didn't matter, though, because we were friends.

Thank you. Thank you for showing so much courage—more than I think I could have ever expected or understood. Thank you for taking the dive to your own reputation to keep me company.

You may not know it, but you changed my life that summer. You taught me to stand up for people, not to believe gossip and lies, to be inclusive rather than exclusive. You taught me to believe in who I am and to become a more loving person. That's a lesson I've tried to hold on to since. Thank you.

Love,
Carrie

# The Blue-Eyed Girl

## BY JOCELYN MAEVE KELLEY

When I was seven years old I met the blue-eyed girl. We stood dripping wet as the cement pool deck sizzled beneath our delicate feet, the skin still soft and smooth, not yet hardened from repeated exposure to the summer elements of sand and surf. We became summer friends but location tore us apart for the school year and we were forced to focus our attention on other kids, classmates with whom we could share our lunches and our secrets on the playground from September to June. But when summer came, the blue-eyed girl and I were friends again. The excitement reached its pinnacle when we found out we would finally be attending the same school, junior high. Sixth grade.

Suddenly our worlds collided and everything that was simple and easy changed. Boys came into the picture and popularity crept into our psyche and the blue-eyed girl did things that set herself apart from everyone else—a fate worse than death when you are thirteen years old. She cried openly when her feelings were hurt, when she was left out at lunch or from birthday parties and sleepovers. She didn't know that pretending to be someone you're not made life easier, or maybe she just refused to accept it. She held on to everything that made her fiercely different: her emotions, her anger, her bossiness and determination. She wore her heart all over her sleeve.

The lunchroom was the center of sixth-grade life. We were set free for one hour to joke and gossip, to laugh and flirt, to whisper and promise secrecy. Our lunch tables were small and crowded, so the decision of where you sat was one of hot contention. Every day we counted down the hours until the lunch bell rang, and when it did, we prayed that today would not be the day we found ourselves left out. We were selfish and we coveted the inclusion that a seat provided us with. We were so thankful if a chair was left available, saved even, that we never cared who the unlucky ones were who found themselves out of luck. It was a teenage version of musical chairs. If we made it into the "group" table, then everything was sunny and life was good—we were still in the game.

But then the game turned ugly. A trip to the guidance counselor and a look at the tears that our seat saving had caused the blue-eyed girl in particular made my heart hurt. I don't know if it was seeing the look of desperation on her face, the sadness that sat deep in her eyes, the crisis swirling around her, but at that moment I made a change. I no longer fought for the coveted seat at the group table. If the blue-eyed girl wasn't included in the lunchroom, then I didn't want to be included, either. If she wasn't invited to the sleepovers, then I didn't want to go. I would love to say it was smooth sailing after that, but it wasn't. I lost friends. I was the subject of notes passed and whispered secrets in the hallway. But the friendship I had with the blue-eyed girl was all I needed.

Maybe life can be easier if you throw out everything that makes you different and unique, but then it's no longer your life. It's something created, imagined, something owned and dictated by a group. I've seen both sides. I've been inside and I've been out. I chose out. I stepped away from the lunch table. The blue-eyed girl and I found our own seats, apart from the crowd. I walked away from safety and made memories of my own choosing, just me and the blue-eyed girl. Our friendship grew and strengthened over the years. We became an inseparable duo. It took us through the hallways of high school, the campus visits of college, and the bars of our early twenties. When I would run into some of those girls from the "popular" lunch table, they told me that if I hadn't been friends with the blue-eyed girl, they would have included me. I couldn't have cared less. I stood up for the one left behind. I willingly jumped into the fire, and yes, my feet got burned, but I kept walking and have never looked back.

# Frenemies Are Not Friends

## BY MICHELLE ZINK

My daughter's bullies came disguised as friends.

It started at the end of seventh grade, but to understand it all, you have to go back further than that.

Pretty much from birth, my daughter was an attention getter. It might have been the blond hair and green eyes, or it might have been her utter disregard for what other people thought—I've learned that confidence is appealing in pretty much everyone.

Who knows?

What I do know is that she didn't strive for it. She just did things the way she wanted to, without a thought to what anyone would think. She wore clothing in strange combinations (something I attributed to artistic tendencies that were later proven), experimented with weird hairstyles starting in kindergarten, and sat down in the middle of the soccer field during games because "My legs are so tired, Mommy." Even when her teammates yelled and screamed, angry that they might lose because of her lack of effort, no amount of cajoling could convince her to play when the truth was, she just didn't want to.

Once, while rehearsing the day before a dance recital, she sat down on the stage as the other girls twirled around her, casting astonished glances her way amid shouts of "You're ruining *everything!*" Afterward, I asked her why she would behave in such a way right before a recital.

"Tomorrow you'll be onstage in front of lots and lots of people, honey. Don't you care that you might not be ready?"

She thought about the question long enough for me to know she was actually considering it before replying, "No."

I was stunned. *How can she not* care? I thought. What about the other girls, who were counting on her? What about her teacher, who would or would not recommend that she be moved into the advanced class next session?

But then I realized how incredible it would be *not to care.* To be so sure of who I was that I did what was right for me without a single thought to what other people would think. I started hoping she could hang on to that feeling, and I was happy when it remained a part of her year after year.

Getting glasses in the third grade seemed to solidify her place as one of the polite, semi-invisible kids in school. Her teacher told me that during free time, she liked to draw or read despite the fact that she did have a small group of good friends. She didn't seem unhappy or shunned, the teacher said.

Just happy to be by herself.

I took it as a good sign. A sign that my daughter was happy within herself and didn't need the validation of a million friends to be happy. She continued to develop selectively close friendships with girls like herself—girls who cared about how they did in school and weren't growing up too fast.

Then, in seventh grade, she decided to get contacts. And it changed everything.

The girls who used to ignore her started saying hello and including her in conversations. The boys for whom she'd been invisible suddenly sat up and took notice. My daughter noticed, too, but in the way I hoped she would.

"Why didn't they pay attention to me before when I had glasses?" she said. "What makes them think I want to be friends with them now when they didn't like who I was before?"

And I would think, *Smart girl.*

But as much as the change in people she didn't know surprised her, the changes in the people she knew surprised her more. Suddenly, the girls with whom she'd been friends for years started whispering behind her back. There were parties to which she wasn't invited, and any boy for whom she expressed interest—no matter how much he had been previously derided—was suddenly a target for her "friends."

The situation quickly degenerated to an aggressive rumor campaign and, finally, to my daughter having her name written on the girls' bathroom wall in conjunction with something truly humiliating by someone who had once been her very best friend.

This time she cared.

As someone who'd spent her entire childhood and adolescence within a circle of trusted friends, all of them playing it low-key, she was ill prepared for the viciousness that ensued. In her eyes nothing had changed. She was still the same girl she'd always been, but it became commonplace for her to come home in tears. Being targeted and ostracized by the girls she had once trusted was utterly devastating to her.

The girls who had once been her friends inexplicably didn't want to be her friend anymore, and she wasn't interested in joining the ranks of the big-headed, fast-moving kids in the so-called popular crowd who now seemed willing to welcome her. For the first time ever, she felt alone and isolated.

I was at a loss, too. We spent hours talking over the things that happened and all of our possible recourses before agreeing it would be best to try to let it go. To move on to something better.

And I think it took awhile, even for me, to recognize it as the bullying that it was. Perpetrated by the people my daughter had always known, it was insidious and vague. She wasn't pushed or physically abused. She wasn't forced to do things she didn't want to do.

But school became a scary and confusing place. Those who knew her best used what they knew to hurt her. They made it their business to keep her down and do all they could to ensure that she was alienated and unhappy.

There were more changes over the summer between seventh and eighth grade. My daughter got taller and slimmer. She blossomed. Even adults she'd known her whole life didn't recognize her until someone said her name.

Which was pretty much the nail in the coffin of all her old friendships.

But the good news is that she gained some other things, too. With a little encouragement, she hosted several summer get-togethers, making a point to invite people she didn't know very well. Our methods for choosing invitees were . . . unconventional! We took a yearbook and went down the list of every single person in her grade. It went something like this:

Me: "Who's this?"

Her: "Oh, that's Heather."

Me: "What's her story?"

Her: "She's weird."

Me: "Weird, how?"

Her: "I don't know. She doesn't talk much. And I don't really even see her at lunch or anything. But she's a really good artist."

Me: "Really? Well, you like art. Is she nice?"

Her: "Yeah."

Me: "Is she a troublemaker or something?"

Her: "No . . ."

Me: "Maybe she just hasn't found her place yet. Think we should invite her?"

Her: "Okay. I could try."

And so it went.

It was an odd assortment at first! We ended up with people from every crowd who had only one thing in common—my daughter thought they were all nice, interesting people. Like her, many of them were adrift, and they found kinship in their shared search for friendships they could count on.

I was proud of her. It was a gutsy move. She was already a little shy, and it was scary to call people she didn't know very well and invite them to a party. Plus, they didn't all come.

But some of them did, and a funny thing grew out of those first awkward parties.

Friendship. The real kind. The kind where you have shared values and interests. The kind where you want one another to thrive and be happy.

My daughter is sixteen now and many of those friends are still a part of her life. Those days—the ones where she had to steel herself to go to school in the morning and try not to cry until she arrived home—seem far away. She looks back on them with a mixture of surprise and horror. I think time and distance have softened the memory, but I still see her shudder when someone mentions a particularly brutal episode.

Yet for all its brutality, she learned something valuable. She learned that even those dark and terrible moments that are embedded in our psyche change and fade. That the world is not as small as it can seem. That there are people in it who will hurt you to ease their own pain, insecurity, and fear.

But if you look a little closer, there are people in it who are like you, too. People who will love and accept and cherish you as you are. Often, you will find them in the most unexpected places.

And when you get right down to it, that's really what life is: one long opportunity to find "your" people. The ones who make your world a better place and the ones for whom you can make the world a little brighter as well.

Every day is another chance. Another opportunity to find them.

You just have to do your part. You just have to keep looking.

# INSIGHT

# The Other Side
## BY NANCY HOLDER

Recently, I received a letter brimming with pain and remorse. It was from a bully. "I'm the queen bee you've written about," she wrote. "I'm the one people save a seat for and hope I'll sit down next to them in return. I'm the one with the cool clothes and I throw the good parties. People want to hang out with me. They do all kinds of things just to be seen with me. But I'm mean, and my friends are mean, and I don't know how to stop."

I told her that I know how that feels.

When I was in middle school, I was the kind of girl who was "good" popular—president of the Associated Student Body, editor of the paper, friend to all . . . or so they thought. But I gleefully filled out the pages of a slam book with dozens of names in it, and not all my comments were nice.

Some were far from nice. Some were very, very mean. With some years between then and now, I'm stunned that I could have said such things. But at the time, we scribbled in that book in classes, passing it around when the teachers weren't looking. We worked on it during lunch. *Gross, zitty, BO.* Some of my disses were classics of snark, or so I imagined: *B-O-B = L-S-R.* As if every mean thing I wrote were some soaring haiku of wit. *SUL SUX.*

At the end of the week that the slam book made its rounds, I got called to the principal's office. I sat across from his gray metal desk in a sweat while he asked me if, in my position as the school president and the newspaper editor, I could put a stop to cruel, mean-spirited things like this. Maybe I could write an editorial. Or I could give a speech at the next pep rally. He was genuinely distressed and disappointed that "some people" could turn against their fellow students like wild animals and display such a lack of respect and regard for common decency. As he paged through the spiral-bound notebook, shaking his head, he talked about how some of these insults and digs might stick with the victims for the rest of their lives.

Since we had each created a symbol to represent our names, he didn't know I had taken part. Was I ashamed that I wrote in the slam book? Yes, but that shame came much later. When I sat there in his office, I didn't feel so much remorse as acute terror that I would be busted. I was more worried about getting in trouble than I was about inflicting lasting damage on anyone's psyche.

The Dalai Lama said, "Be kind whenever possible. It is always possible." And Plato said, "Be kind, for everyone you meet is fighting a hard battle." But I know that when you're scoring points for epic put-downs and clever repartee, it's hard to remember to be kind. When you're in the passenger seat and the driver, aka your best friend, rolls up the windows because *that* girl starts walking toward the car—that mousy chick with the bad skin, who's maybe hoping just to say "Hi" to you because you've got everything and you're so pretty, it's so easy to forget. It's much easier to remember that you have a reputation to preserve, and you sure don't want to get stuck with this loser—be nice for two seconds, and she'll be inviting you to the movies, just watch. Easiest of all to make a point of locking the windows and doors and shouting "Let's get out of here!" instead of giving zit-chick a wave—a place in the sun, two seconds of your time.

My letter writer sounded just as sad and confused as anyone who's ever been picked on. And just as powerless. The center of attention, the reigning queen of school, and she had a slam-book-style secret. She didn't want the power to hurt.

The Dalai Lama also said, "If you want to be happy, practice compassion. If you want others to be happy, practice compassion." I told that queen bee to start forgiving herself, first and foremost. Over time, the bully inside her will lose its favorite target. And then she'll get her real power back.

Maybe someone could help her with that.

# Can We Make This Letter Disappear?

## BY SARA BENNETT WEALER

Hi, Sara—

It's Sara. Not Sara from English class or Sarah from choir. It's actually you—Sara—writing from the future. That sentence felt really weird to write, so I can imagine what you're thinking: Is this a joke? Did I somehow get cast in a cheesy sci-fi movie? This isn't some new reality TV show, Sara; this really is you, twenty years from now.

I know. I wouldn't believe it either, so here's proof: (1) You're not exactly sure *what* happened with that guy you met last summer at the lake, but it kind of scared you and you haven't told anyone about it. And (2) You're secretly terrified those spots on the back of your leg are cancer. (Don't worry, they aren't.)

I hope I haven't freaked you out. Actually, if anybody

should be freaking out, it's me. When I signed on to write this letter, I got a warning that any information I shared with the past could affect the present in unforeseen and dramatic ways. I think we're okay, though, because I've been careful not to reveal anything that could change how things turn out. You might like to know that your life—at least as far as I've lived it—turns out pretty great, and there isn't all that much that I would change.

Except for one thing.

That's the reason I'm writing. But I'm not sure it will make sense if I just blurt it out, so I'm going to ease in with a few lessons I've learned over the years—stuff I wish someone would have told me when I was sixteen.

**That guy? So not worth fighting over.** I know you've had problems with girls. I know not all of it has to do with guys, but let's be honest: guys are a major reason girls are nasty to each other. "Is that girl trying to steal my guy?" "Does the guy I like like that girl better?" "Who does that girl think she is?" Sara, believe me when I tell you that *no* guy is worth getting involved in a big, hairy drama. There are literally millions of boys out there, and the world would be a much nicer place if more girls said, "Next!" the minute they got a hint that a guy was interested in someone else. Because that says something about him, *not* the other girl. Instead of tormenting her, concentrate on finding a better guy. They're out there (and guess what . . . you're going to marry one).

**That girl you make fun of? She's the cool one at cocktail parties.** You know how you dream about getting out of Kansas and being a sophisticated adult? Well, when you start going to real parties—the kind where they don't drink beer out of plastic cups—you'll be surprised to see who everybody wants to talk with. It's that girl you called a freak—the one who dresses weird and listens to music you don't like. She and her friends are into stuff like art and drama, which you're into, too, but you downplay because the people you're friends with think it's stupid and you don't want to be called a freak as well. Here's the thing, though: what makes those girls weird now will make them fascinating in a few years. They'll have the great stories, the awesome style, and you'll be scrambling to be more like them. So quit making fun, stop worrying what other people think, and start being more fascinating yourself.

**Those girls who make fun of you? They might end up unhappy—or they might not.** This is what you tell yourself when the in-crowd crap gets to you: they'd better enjoy it now because they're going to wind up unfulfilled nobodies who never left high school. In some cases that's true. From what I've been able to tell, some of your former classmates do appear to be stuck in senior year. Others, though, will grow up to be super fabulous. The truth is that mean kids can turn into successful (sometimes still mean) adults. They'll be your neighbors, your coworkers—maybe even your bosses. So learn to get along with them now. Practice being diplomatic but not underhanded, honest but not catty, friendly yet smart and guarded. You don't have to be fake—if someone's not a good friend, then nothing you can do will change that. But hiding isn't an option, and neither is being mean back.

**Because being mean? That's called bullying.** You're lucky; you've never been tormented or threatened on a regular basis. But the infighting, the bitchy remarks, the little ways that girls can cut one another down? That's bullying, too. And you've done it just as often as you've had it done to you. You might not have realized it at first. It can be so subtle, so easy, and sometimes it feels so good to be the one who's got the gossip, the one who's on the inside, the one who is *not* being laughed at or left out. But if you know you're hurting someone, then it's bullying. And the damage doesn't go away. It will come back in ways you can't possibly imagine now. But I'm going to help you imagine it because . . .

**Your daughter is counting on you.** This is it—the one thing I would never change and yet would alter the world for. I won't give details because I don't want to take a chance that, by knowing too much, you might somehow do something that could cause you not to have her. All I will tell you is that your little girl is more wonderful than you could ever imagine and that you will be proud of her in a million different ways each and every day of her life.

And it will break your heart.

Because a child blossoms so gradually and intimately that you come to know every expression and emotion as if it were your own. And just when you're watching her step into the world, full of the self-loving confidence that every person deserves to feel, you'll watch her meet the brick wall of a bully. Someone will say, "I don't like you." Or they'll run away or gather up other kids against her. You'll recognize immediately what's going on; she won't. She'll try again. She'll be shocked, stung, and then you'll see it start to sink in.

Playground politics will morph into parties she's not invited to; groups she's included in one day, then excluded from the next; critiques of her clothes, her hair, her body. You'll see her build up the defenses that you recognize so well and you'll think, *How dare they do this to her?* Then you'll remember all the times *you* judged someone. The times you froze another girl out. And you will pray that she never experiences what you did, but you know she will, and you'll know you can't save her from it.

I'm telling you this knowing it may be impossible for you to understand. You're nowhere near ready to imagine what it's like to be a mother. But what if you do think about it? What if some small shift in you causes a shift in someone else? Could that echo twenty years into the future?

It's a chance I want to take, for our little girl.

So I'm signing off and sending this letter. And then I'll wait and watch. Will she become more confident? Will I know better how to help her? Will I even remember that I contacted you, because, when I wake up tomorrow, she and I will have changed in such a way that what happened today no longer exists? You're a good person; so are your friends— and things get complicated, I know. But what I hope, with all my heart, is that you'll look to the future now, so you won't regret the past later.

Good luck, Sara. Enjoy what's to come. (And try harder in math—trust me on this!)

With much love,
Sara

# Bully on the Ledge

## BY KURTIS SCALETTA

I was the new kid seven times between first and twelfth grades. In every year but one, I was the smallest boy in my class. Not only was I smart, I was a smart-ass. I made fun of other kids when they used words wrong or got their facts mixed up. I made fun of the *teacher* when she used words wrong or got her facts mixed up.

I read from big, thick books. They were nothing special, but they looked show-off-y to other kids. They'd say I was faking and make me read passages from them to prove I could. Then they would say I was making it up anyway. In fourth grade, I read *The Shining*. It was pretty accessible and had a child hero I could identify with. Some other boys made me read a page, and there was a bad word on it. They ran to the teacher and told her I'd said a swear word. She took the book away from me.

Kids would say my name in a mean way as they rode by me on their bikes. "Scaletta!" they would say, like it was a bad word. They'd take things from me and hold them out of reach. They'd ask me if I was going to cry, and sometimes I did.

I was almost always the last one picked for sports teams, but I understood—I was small and ineffective. Once the kid who passed on me apologized later. It was a sign of real respect, and of slowly realized social acceptance. When I got glasses, some kids tossed them back and forth over my head. When someone finally threw them back to me and I dropped them, and they broke, he was genuinely sorry.

Over time those kids would become at least casual friends. It turned out I was fast for a short distance, and other kids would want to race me. I knew a lot of jokes. Most important, I was a red-blooded, straight, white, Christian, able-bodied and able-minded male. While I was different, I was still "one of them." I occupied a space of marginal acceptability, like a small wolf from a different pack, but eventually I made my way into the hierarchy. There were lesser wolves than me, and there was prey.

Only one kid did have an especially intense hatred for me. That came in middle school. He put mean notes in my coat, calling me a racist name. I wasn't black, but I had curly hair, and that was all he needed. I expect he would have rather had a real minority to harass, but our class didn't have any that year. He challenged me to fights after school. He finally forced me to, and I won, thanks to guile and a patch of ice. I got him backed helplessly against the ledge of a window well, scooped up his legs, and threatened to let go. He cried and begged other kids to help. None of them did. I helped him back to safety, supposing my mercy would give way to a robust new friendship. It didn't, and no wonder. I'd humiliated him, not just because he lost, but because not one kid would team up against a weakling to help him. Now he's the sort of guy who goes to political rallies with misspelled signs.

I'm not ashamed of having been bullied. A few hardships made me. I'm more liberal-minded because of them and more inclined to side with the underdog.

My shame is having ever joined in the abuse. I realized once there was a kid who, though taller than me, could be rabbit punched and tweaked without fighting back. Another time I made a racist joke in the locker room and, during the same spell, told an anti-Semitic joke on the bus, loud enough for the sole Jewish kid to hear. There was the time I joined in a round of teasing of a friend when we discovered he suffered from a weird, mostly harmless but embarrassing medical problem. And the time I abandoned a new friend because nobody else liked her. There were a dozen times that I faked a smile while my not-quite-friends savaged an overweight girl, and a hundred times I tuned out their derision for the kid everyone suspected was gay. I felt powerless to make a difference, anyway, and would rather be on the side that was winning. I think about all those incidents all the time. They're the ones that bother me to look back on—those times that I showed my meanness and cowardice. They also made me who I am today. If I hadn't been small or smart or the new kid—or even if I'd been only two of those three—I might have had a thousand such moments, and they'd have made me into a different man. I'd be less thoughtful, less inclined to side with victims. I might not be as literate. I'd be the one taking misspelled signs to political rallies.

Everything you do as a kid adds up to who you are as an adult. Your experiences and decisions are a column of red and black numbers. If you want to be the grown-up you can be proud of, take the hard times in good humor. Make the hard times of others softer. Pull the bully back from the ledge.

# Informed Consent

## BY LARA ZEISES

*September 13, 1990*

*I don't want this. I don't want people picking on me & I don't want to be fat . . . I just want to be me.*

Here's one of my earliest memories: I was standing in my grandparents' bedroom, in front of the full-length mirror that hung on their closet door, looking at my naked body. I was supposed to be trying on clothes they'd gotten me, but instead I was pinching my stomach and crying. I thought, *Why do I have to be so* fat?

I was four years old.

The worst part? I wasn't even fat (yet). Chunky, maybe. Chubby at best.

That didn't make a lick of difference to Tony*, the

_____

* Names have been changed to protect the not-so-innocent.

classmate from kindergarten who insisted on teasing me. Every. Single. Day. I wasn't Tony's only target; he was pretty much an equal-opportunity offender. Nor was he the only school-yard bully I'd have to deal with between kindergarten and my high school graduation. But to this day, I remember his face with crystal precision. And to this day, I still want to slap the shit-eating grin off his smug little mug.

It's no secret that fat kids attract some of the worst bullies. Probably because hating on fatties is one of the last socially acceptable forms of prejudice. Even today, when more than 50 percent of Americans are classified as obese, it's still considered basically okay to make fun of a kid who shops in the plus-size department. Fat people are fat because they eat too much. Fat people are fat because they don't get enough exercise. Fat people are fat because . . . well, does it even matter? Fat is bad, thin is good, and if you're the former instead of the latter, then it's probably your own fault.

This was what I thought for most of my young adult life. That I was fat because I didn't have any willpower. That I was fat because I was lazy. This was what I was told by . . . well, by everybody. So I believed it. Mostly.

Throughout middle and high school, there were a lot of people who made fun of me because of my weight. But there are two I'll never, ever forget: Alex and Henry Short.

The Short brothers were not, in fact, short. Henry was super tall and super skinny. His brother, Alex, was of average height and kind of stocky in an athletic sort of way. I tried to stay as far off their radar as possible, but we went to the same small private school, and there were less than thirty-five students in our entire grade. If the Short brothers wanted to make your life hell, there wasn't a whole lot you could do about it.

I spent the first two years of high school trying to pretend that their constant taunts didn't hurt me. They liked to refer to me as the Stay Puft Marshmallow Man—as in the super-huge, sugar-spun "villain" of the movie *Ghostbusters*. They'd make booming noises whenever I walked. If their comments about my weight weren't riling me up enough, they'd start in on my clothes, my glasses, my hair.

The summer after my sophomore year, I transferred to a large public school and, thankfully, never had to deal with the Short brothers again. But I never forgot about them. And I certainly never forgave them.

Then, one recent night, through the magic portal that is Facebook, I actually found Alex Short. *The* Alex Short. And me being me, I couldn't resist the opportunity to send him a message. It went something like, *Hi, you and your douche bag brother were really mean to me, and now I'm a successful author and you're not.* If I'm going to be completely honest, my message was a whole lot nastier, but that's not entirely relevant. Because here's the thing:

*Alex Short didn't remember me.*

At first, I didn't believe him. I wrote back, expanding

on all of the terrible names I remembered him and Henry calling me. Alex apologized. I didn't buy that apology, so I wrote him again, laying into him even harder. Finally, he responded:

I feel even more like an absolute douche bag for not remembering [because] taunting someone like you say we [did] is WRONG! I have done some screwed up things in my life and karma has seen to it that I get paid back. I DO apologize and wish you the best in life. I again congratulate you on your success. It is good to see you take the negative and change it to a positive. You should be commended over and over! Again, good luck!

I. Was. Speechless.

I was also quite embarrassed. I mean, here I was, spewing out some ugly, hateful words to a boy I hadn't even *seen* in more than fifteen years. And there he was, offering what ultimately seemed like a sincere apology for some stupid things he said when he was a mere teenager. Things he didn't remember saying to a girl he didn't remember. Period.

How is it possible that I had every detail of our biology classroom burned into my brain, down to which desk I sat in as he and Henry sang out, "Who you gonna call?" over and over and over again, but Alex Short didn't so much as remember my *name*? How? Seriously, how?

I don't know how. I really don't.

But here's the thing: in the end, it doesn't really matter.

Kids are mean. Kids are cruel. But the sad truth is, *I* was my own worst bully.

It's true. *I* was the one whose cheeks flushed red whenever the Short brothers serenaded me with the *Ghostbusters* theme song. *I* was the one who let their voices get inside my head— who let their voices stay there for so many years, long after I'd fallen out of their collective consciousness.

Adults will tell you that bullies are only as powerful as you let them be. And when you're a teenager, you'll think they're full of shit. I know I did.

But in the end? They're right, you know. It's like that quote from Eleanor Roosevelt: "No one can make you feel inferior without your consent."

So don't give it to them. After all, there's a good chance they won't even remember that you did.

# Silent All These Years

## BY ALYSON NOËL

It started the moment I stepped onto the bus.

The sidelong glances. The not-so-hushed whispers.

"New girl."

"The one who moved into *that* house."

Words directed at the back of my head as I claimed the first available seat. Aware of them leaning over one another, craning their necks, widening their eyes, hoping to see something they could add to the story they were already forming.

Something worth talking about.

I fought to overcome my shyness. Forced myself to look around and smile. Tried to work past the nervous twitch in my belly, to look accommodating and friendly. My efforts were met by curious looks, piercing glares, dissecting stares— causing me to hunker down and retreat, keeping quiet, keeping to myself, staring out the window, praying it soon would be over.

A long, bumpy ride on a bus with bad shocks.

A quick trip to the office and then on to class with a pink slip clutched in my fist.

An awkward introduction in which I was forced to stand before the chalkboard, stand before my new classmates, stating my full name and where I'd moved from, while my gut clenched so badly and my face turned so red, I swung my long brown hair before me, hoping I could somehow hide behind it, pretend I wasn't really there.

A move I'd soon learn to regret.

A move that haunted me for the next five years.

"Did you see the way she *swung* her hair?"

"Did you know she lives in *that* house?"

And by lunch, a group of older girls, girls who were ten to my nine, had taken it upon themselves to rename me.

No longer Alyson.

No longer "new girl."

"Stuck-up Bitch" is what they called me.

They even created a song to go with it—one that made liberal use of my new name, accompanied by lots of hair tossing.

But despite the lyrics professing that I thought I was "*sooo bitchin'*," I'm here to say I felt anything but.

I may have lived in the biggest house in the neighborhood, I may have had long hair and nice clothes, but all of that was just a Band-Aid meant to cover the truth.

My life was a mess.

I was the poster child for low self-esteem.

And despite the big house, I soon would be poor.

With parents on the verge of divorce, a mom struggling to deal with the demise of everything she'd known for the past twenty years, and a dad who, on the rare occasions he chose to come home, made it a point to either berate me or ignore me, my entire world was collapsing to the point where my home life and my school life became mirrors of each other. Making it impossible to determine which was more miserable.

The stomachaches were getting so bad I started coming home early, until one day, feeling particularly overwhelmed by it all, I mentioned the bullying, the name that they called me, only to be told to ignore it. If I ignored it they'd soon move on to something else.

But ignoring it didn't work. If anything it just made them sing louder. So I kept quiet. Didn't mention it again.

Mostly because I felt ashamed.

When an entire group of kids decides to reject you at first sight, without talking to you or getting to know you, without giving you a chance to prove yourself—it does more than just hurt, it makes you question your entire being, your self-worth.

Those were the days when nobody spoke about bullying. It was something boys did. Primal. Survival of the fittest.

Perfectly normal. Kids will be kids. Easily handled with a shrug, a look the other way, a mumbled comment about soon growing out of it and moving on to better things.

And certainly no one acknowledged that girls were capable of it. Capable of crafting a systematic form of social terrorism that consisted of snide looks, passed notes, and whispered insults when adults and teachers were present—progressing when they weren't to outright lies, rumors, physical aggression, and, in my case, a horrible song I couldn't escape.

They sang it on the bus. Sang it during recess, and again during lunch. Sang it when they passed by my house after school, and on weekends, too. After a while they even grew bold enough to sing it right out in the open, in front of my teacher, who shrugged, looked the other way, pretended not to hear.

By eighth grade it was over.

After five solid years, it seemed they'd finally grown bored and moved on. But while the taunting may have ended, the effects lingered for much longer than I care to admit. And I always swore that if I ever got published, I'd write a book about a girl who experiences something similar in the hope that my experience might help someone else. That book turned out to be my second novel, *Art Geeks and Prom Queens*.

And though it seems like this story is over, there's still

one last bit left to tell. About a year ago, completely out of the blue, one of my bullies sent me an email.

She wanted to apologize, to tell me how horrible she felt for the way she'd chosen to treat me back then. Having kids of her own, she could hardly believe what she'd done. It was the sort of thing she'd never tolerate from them. And though she tried, she couldn't really answer the *why*. I was new, had long hair, had a big house—at the time, it seemed like enough.

When I read her message, I was shocked by how much I still cared. I'd come a long way since those days, was enjoying a life I'd worked very hard to create. I took my time with it, chose to revisit it over the course of several days. Determined to deal with the swarm of long-buried emotions that came rushing back, emotions I sought to get a handle on before I hit reply.

And in my reply I forgave her.

I forgave her because doing so freed me from the burden of that particular past.

I forgave her because I had no good reason not to.

It takes a whole lot of courage to own up to something like that, and when her former partner in crime also emailed an apology, I forgave her as well.

And after all of that, this is what I want to leave you with:

If you're being bullied—speak up! You do not have to suffer in silence. Tell an adult, a relative, a friend, someone you can trust to help you deal with it.

If you are the bully—*stop it*! Just *stop it*. Right now.

Building yourself up at someone else's expense is one of the lowliest acts you can ever commit.

There is no excuse.

It is *never* okay to engage in that way.

And if bullying is something you've done in your past, then keep in mind that it's never too late to apologize— no matter how many decades have passed. I can say from experience that the sentiment goes a very long way.

Choose kindness.

Be well.

Peace. Joy. Love.

# Now and Then

## BY APRILYNNE PIKE

"Fight! Fight! Fight! Fight!"

It was a sound I dreaded. Not that I was ever in the fight, but I hated the sight of kids my age beating on each other. I couldn't imagine ever hitting anyone once, much less over and over the way I saw some fights proceed. I despise violence. Even now I have trouble watching realistic violence in movies. So throughout my younger years, when the age-old chant broke out at school, you could expect me to be the one heading not toward the crowd but for the nearest classroom to tell the teacher. And I don't feel an ounce of shame over that.

On the other hand, verbal torment has always been a part of my life. I could hardly have avoided it; I was a poster child for nerdiness. I got glasses in kindergarten—big, thick Coke-bottle glasses with those terrible plastic eighties frames—loved to wear my hair in two braids, made friends with teachers more easily than with my peers, and was a moony, easily distracted little thing. I was teased for everything. My homemade clothes, which I loved. The book that was always in my face, which I now consider a wise investment in my future career! In middle school I was teased and shunned for being a lesbian—even though I'm not. And, like most girls, I went through the cycle of being teased both for not having breasts and, later, for having them. (I always had to scratch my head at that.)

But through all of that, I always had the thought: *At least no one's beating me up.* It was my greatest fear.

I remember looking forward to turning eighteen, moving out, and going to college because, of course, bullying stops once you get out of high school.

Everyone take a moment to laugh with me.

Turns out, bullies don't go away. They just change. Instead of kids who are physically bigger than you wanting your lunch money, you have arrogant jerks who think they're smarter than you or better than you, who want your job or your life or just to make themselves feel bigger by making you feel small. And you know what? They still don't like that I'm a nerd. Some things never change.

There aren't nearly as many *physical* bullies once you're an adult—that is true. You don't often hear about fistfights at the office or stories of everyone gathering in a circle at the grocery store and shoving the person in the middle around, like kids used to do on the playground.

But sometimes I think I'd rather have someone just punch me in the face. Not only would it be over quickly but it would be easy to point my finger and say, "Hey! That person is bullying me!" (And the ability to get the law on my side wouldn't hurt, either.) Over the years, I've had a friend try to undermine my career, a religious leader with a strange need to prove how important he was, even a coworker who went to rather extreme lengths to let the world know how much she hated me.

And you know what's crazy? If I were to confront any of these people and tell them I didn't appreciate being bullied, I suspect they would all honestly deny that they were being bullies at all. Despite their exhibiting all the classic signs and tactics of bullies, I don't think any of these people are aware of what they're doing.

Adult bullying can be so subtle. But when it happens, I know my first reaction is to curl into myself and slouch by and escape as soon as possible, just like I did when I was a kid. I don't. I've learned some skills since I was ten. But on the inside, I feel the same—the same bewilderment, the same hurt. Why would someone treat me this way? That part hasn't changed in twenty years. I don't know that it ever changes.

I picked up my daughter from school the other day and she reported with wide eyes that one of her friends confided in her that she was afraid to walk home because a bully would be waiting to beat her up. My daughter was understandably very concerned—and fortunately, the incident did not actually end up happening. Still, after telling her that she should let a teacher know if her friend ever told her something like that again (I have no problem being the narc), I started to think about the bullying my daughter will surely face in the upcoming years.

She's already one of those "smart kids," having skipped a grade. Strike one. She wears glasses just like I did (though, I admit, hers are much thinner and cuter than mine ever were). Strike two. And guess who makes the skirts she loves to wear to school? My mother; the same woman who made my clothes in any pattern and color I wanted when I was little. Strike three. There will be teasing, there will be torment, and I suspect there will be nights of her crying on my lap the same way I did with my mom.

I hope she gets through it. I see a boldness in her that I never had, and that gives me hope. But you know what I hope most of all? That I can teach her to never stoop to their level. To never become a bully herself—even as an adult. I want her to be aware of when she is hurting other people. Because simply teaching her not to punch her classmates isn't enough. I want to teach her to care and be tolerant. Because if you don't learn that as a kid, you have a whole lifetime for that bullying streak to come to the surface.

Because it doesn't end with high school. But maybe it can end with us.

# Strangers on a Street

## BY DIANA RODRIGUEZ WALLACH

A couple of years ago, while I was planning my wedding, I came face-to-face with the girl who destroyed my life in sixth grade. She stopped me on the street, sweet as candy, and asked how I was doing. She cooed over my engagement ring, inquired about where I was working, and asked how my parents were doing. Everything was smiles and hugs; she was thrilled to have "run into me."

I'd like to tell you that I was happy to see her, too, that I was delighted she was doing great at her job, and that I was genuinely sincere when I wished her well with her own wedding plans. I know that was what I was supposed to be feeling. (It was what I said, after all. You know, the "right" thing, the "polite" thing.) But I didn't mean a word of it. A little piece of me still hopes her hair falls out one day.

You see, this girl wasn't just a mean girl. She wasn't a queen bee or a Lindsay Lohan stereotype.

She was my best friend. My first friend in the entire world.

Until she dumped me.

We'd been best friends since second grade, five years (which, in adolescent years, is like five hundred), and I never saw the end coming. There was no big fight, no betrayal, no boy we were competing for, or any academic or athletic rivalries on the line.

One day we were best friends, spending our half day from school roller-skating in my basement (yes, we did that back then). The next day she was calling me on the phone telling me that she didn't want to be my best friend anymore. The conversation lasted only seconds, and she never gave a reason. (Though, when you're being dumped, is there ever a rationale that you'll accept?)

Our friendship simply ended. And if that were the extent of what happened, I probably would have been devastated at the loss of her friendship, but I wouldn't be writing this essay.

Unfortunately, Amanda's* decision to cut me from her life ultimately set a chain of events in motion that ended with our "friends," all beautiful, popular cheerleaders (yes, I

---

* Names have been changed. Obviously. But I'm sure if "Amanda" were ever to read this, she'd know this essay is about her . . .

was part of *that* group), launching a full-scale attack.

It lasted a week. Five school days.

That might not seem like a long time, but when you're being chased from class to class by a mob of powerful girls screaming "Bitch! Skank! Loser!" loud enough for your four hundred classmates to hear, you can feel like you're in a time-lapse horror movie.

And the worst part was I suffered in silence, utter isolation. I didn't tell my parents. I didn't tell my sister. I obviously didn't have any friends to talk to about the situation. I didn't even write it in my diary. It was as if the situation was too embarrassing, too painful, even to admit to myself in writing, so instead a four-month gap exists in my journal from that year.

Somehow I even managed to be publicly stoned every forty-one minutes, between every class period, without a single teacher noticing.

Well, wait, that isn't entirely true.

Around day five, after successfully ignoring these girls, never sputtering a word in defense or shedding a tear in their presence, I finally broke. I couldn't breathe, my chest was cracking from the pressure of their insults, and I entered my math class in sobs.

My teacher pulled me into the hall, demanding to know the problem, and while I didn't want to rat (is there anything worse a twelve-year-old can do?), I needed to talk. So I confessed what I was going through, tears streaking my cheeks, nose running, until the teacher cut me off, a finger pointed in my face. "Diana, pull yourself together!" she snapped, then marched me back into her classroom.

Eventually, I found new friends, a new lunch table to sit at, and new bonds that have lasted to this day. Three of the bridesmaids at my wedding were friends I've had since middle or high school.

But the scars of that week have remained, and I don't say this lightly.

As an adult, I can tell you that my relationships with women have been affected by that sixth-grade experience. As recently as a couple of years ago, I realized that I still get nervous when a friend doesn't call me back (maybe she's mad at me?) or when we heatedly disagree on social/political/family issues (what if we stop being friends over this?). It took me a while to identify where these extreme worries were coming from, why that sick pit in my stomach always jumped to the worst conclusion to even the most minor negative occurrence between me and a female friend.

And it is because when I was twelve years old, that was exactly what happened.

I lost my best friend over nothing. I didn't do anything to her, and there was nothing I could have done to prevent it—other than being an entirely different person, because it wasn't an action of mine she was rejecting, it was *me*. She moved on to a "cooler" best friend. We never spoke again.

Somehow, until the day we graduated, we managed to be on the same sports teams, walk through the same halls, go to the same dances, and attend some of the same classes, and never share a word, never let our eyes meet. We were strangers; those five years of our lives never happened, like deleted memories. I was easily forgettable.

And then I saw her on the street. I was actually writing a book about bullying at the time (a book I'm still working on), and the memories of that ordeal were so fresh it was as if I had drawn her to me with my writing. I saw her twice more after that in the span of six months. She bought a house seven blocks from mine. Her husband joined my gym.

And I'd like to say that the universe brought her to me to learn some big lesson, but if that's true, I'm not sure I absorbed it. Each time I saw her, I didn't want to speak to her, I didn't miraculously forget everything that happened, and I wasn't happy to reminisce about the good ol' days. But still I smiled, I nodded, I acted interested. That could not have been the lesson: to be inauthentic? But I also doubt the lesson was that I should have confronted her on the street with something that happened twenty years ago, either.

Maybe the lesson was to confront the fact that there is a name for what I went through at that time, a name I never used until now. I was *bullied*. And I survived it.

You might hate it when adults tell you this, but with two

decades separating me from this experience, I can honestly say that the best revenge really is living well. I'm thrilled to go to class reunions now, because I know I'm not the same mousy person I was back then. I'm proud of who I turned out to be, because of and in spite of everything that happened to me growing up. Plus, I wrote a book about the ordeal, so maybe authors really do need to suffer for their art, maybe that's why I so vividly remember what it was like to be a teenager, and maybe that's why I write for young adults now.

So, to the teens who are reading this and are currently being bullied, I say: you will get through it, you will *not* forget it, it *is* a big deal, but hey, maybe one day you can turn it into a great novel. That'll show 'em.

# Objects in Mirror Are More Complex Than They Appear

## BY LAUREN OLIVER

I have a confession to make: I was not bullied in high school. I was not harassed, insulted, humiliated, or ostracized.

At various times, I was, however, the victim of rumors: there was the time when I was a sophomore and I hooked up with a popular junior in front of forty or so of my classmates on a dare; afterward, people shot me dirty looks for weeks, and whispers, snake hisses, followed me down the halls.

Then there was the time as a senior that photos of an (ahem) *intimate* nature made it into the hands of some sophomore boys and managed to circulate throughout almost the entire class before I was able to retrieve them.

But these were blips, minor traumas—not the seismic,

permanent, and isolating ruptures so many teens experience during their high school years. For the most part, things were easy for me. I went to parties. I threw parties. I had friends, had boyfriends (many of them older), and if anything, was probably feared more than fearful: I wasn't always very nice, I am ashamed to say.

Then who was I in high school? To answer that question is also to explain why I wanted to contribute to this anthology. Because there were unquestionably two different me's in high school: there was the me as it was created by others, the me who could be comprehended in, and thus reduced to, a sum of facts and stories (Lauren: *smart, slutty, mean*).

Then there was the me as I understood—or, more accurately, *didn't* understand—myself. And that me was far blurrier, far less easy to categorize. Angry, self-conscious; brave and also desperately insecure; fiercely loyal to my friends; both a partier and a bookworm; promiscuous and deeply ambivalent about sex. I was a soccer player and a smoker, a theater nerd and a lifeguard, a wild child and an impeccable student.

But that description is blurry and full of contradiction, and people have a very limited tolerance for contradiction; and so I remained Lauren: *smart, slutty, mean*.

Humans have a long and not-so-illustrious history of dehumanizing people in order to dominate, subjugate, or otherwise abuse them—from the infamous three-fifths of a person compromise in the US Constitution to our colonizing ancestors' determination that the Native Americans were *savages* to the trials at Salem in the 1600s, in which weird (or promiscuous) women were burned at the stake for being witches.

This is what happens in high school, too: We call people witches. We decide that they are too weird, too different. They are not us.

And then we burn them at the stake. We spread nasty rumors; we call them names; we alienate and ostracize them.

But my point is that the impulses that facilitate this kind of abuse are the same that had me labeled "mean" or, at least briefly, "a slut"; these are the same impulses that also lead us to assign labels like "jock," "theater nerd," "video-game geek": impulses to categorize, to box, to hold desperately to our fragile identities by saying clearly what we are *not*. After all, it has always been easier to understand what we like by virtue of what we don't—anyone who has ever heard the phrase "I like all music except for country!" knows that.

In order to find some solution to the bullying problem, we'll have to be more tolerant of ambiguity, subtlety, and strangeness not just in other people but in *ourselves*. It may be important to your identity that you are a soccer player, but it may be equally important that you can whistle the national anthem backward and make the world's best spicy popcorn and do a wicked impression of Victoria Beckham. Schools, parents, and educational endeavors should encourage people not just to empathize but to discover and celebrate the weirdness in others and in ourselves. We need not just to think but to *live* outside the box. Weirdness is good. It keeps things interesting.

I'll end this essay with a metaphor. Imagine a plate, compartmentalized. In one corner is a pile of plain cooked pasta, lumped together; in another is steamed asparagus; in yet another is a pile of chopped basil; lastly, there is a small pile of feta cheese. The plate is orderly, clean-looking. It is also boring and unappetizing.

But shake things up a little, mix all the ingredients together . . . and, my friends, the miraculous will occur.

I feel I am still very young in many ways, but in the past ten years, since graduating from high school, I have learned several very valuable lessons. I can say with confidence that being kind and generous will make you happier than being mean and withholding; that the only thing worth striving for is individuality; and that celebrating people's differences is, paradoxically, the best way to bring people together.

# SPEAK

# Levels

## BY TANYA LEE STONE

*Being on top is cool*
*especially after working our way up from the bottom*
*But being on top is nothing*
*if you're gonna use it*
*to put people down.*
*I tried to reason with you,*
*talk to you man to man,*
*but you just laughed*
*and kept right on after them.*
*Can't you see they're already scared of you*
*without you acting beneath yourself?*
*They look up to you*
*even though*
*you don't deserve it,*
*looking down from your flimsy cloud.*

*But I'm big enough to tell you*
*and I'm not gonna stop until I get somewhere.*
*What are you going to do about it?*
*I don't care if I piss you off,*
*calling you off*
*those kids.*
*Yeah, we're both on top*
*But you just*
*sunk*
*a little*
*lower.*

# Slivers of Purple Paper
## BY CYN BALOG

Every high school class has one. One person whose name is synonymous with tragedy, whispered with a serious shake of the head or a "tsk, tsk." High school is painful as it is, but for some it's downright torturous. I'm talking about the one who didn't live out the four years, the one for whom all the pressure was just too much.

In my school, that person was Avery.

I had nothing in common with Avery. Avery was smart and athletic and popular, all the things people like me wished we could be. If you put my picture in front of the members of my graduating class, most would probably say they'd never seen me before in their lives. I'd been in the school district since kindergarten, and yet, I was the invisible one. My classmates didn't think of me. They would describe me, if they absolutely *had* to, in one word: *shy*.

How do I know this? Because in seventh grade, my health teacher decided to do a project aimed at boosting our confidence. We arranged our desks in a circle and were each given a little Chinese takeout box and a few scraps of purple construction paper. On top of the boxes, we wrote our names. Every thirty seconds, we had to pass the boxes to the right. It was the job of the others in the circle to write one nice thing about the person whose name was on the box on a piece of purple paper and slip it into her box.

I can't tell you how excited I was when we started this assignment. It was so different from any assignment I'd ever done. We never went around paying one another compliments, and I was dying to see what nice things people thought about me. I'd hoped "generous" and "helpful" and "smart" would be there. Maybe even "nice blue eyes." There was plenty of fodder to fill that box, even if you didn't know me.

I took the assignment as seriously as possible. I'd been made fun of by several of the boys in the class for my giant beak of a nose, and though it was hard to come up with compliments for those people, I managed. "Always speaks his mind" and "Honest" were a few I'd written down. For some, it was easier. It was easy with Avery. We were neighbors, and though I didn't know her well, she was always kind. As I watched her scribbling, I wondered what people would say about her. What kind of amazing box of compliments she would end up with.

Maybe I was being naive, because I learned that day that

seventh graders do not take the opportunity to build up a person when they can instead tear that person down. When I received my box at the end of the assignment, the same word was on each of the twelve sheets of paper, in different ink and handwriting:

*SHY*

I stared at each paper for only a second. Just looking at them hurt. Of course the assignment was nothing but a joke to most of my classmates. How stupid and pointless to praise others when all they'll do in return is shoot you down! After all, I just looked like an idiot throwing all these compliments at people who didn't think anything of me. I was about to stuff the whole thing into my backpack when I pulled out the last slip of paper:

*She might not say much, but when she does speak, she always says something special.*

There it was. The reason that I still remembered that assignment, though so many years had passed. Because I took that sliver of paper and stuck it on my bulletin board at home. As a reminder that I meant something. That I was special. I looked at it every day during high school.

Five years later, Avery killed herself. It was shortly after high school graduation. Nobody knew why. It was one of those big mysteries; even her closest friends shrugged and complained about the senselessness of it all.

A few years after that, her mother finally got around to cleaning out her room. Avery had a lot of books, and her mother thought I might like them. When I went up to her room, I noticed all the trophies and awards. She was a great student and athlete, and I couldn't believe that with all these things that screamed how special she was, she could still feel that life wasn't worth living. I ran my eyes over the room, stopping at her bulletin board. There was a sliver of purple construction paper. On it, I recognized my own handwriting.

*Lights up every room she enters with her effervescent personality.*

Who knows what the other people in class had said. She'd kept mine. It had meant something to her. Only then did I know that she was the one who had written the compliment that I'd saved. She was the only other person who had taken the assignment seriously. It made me wonder whether, if she had received more of those purple papers throughout her life, things would have been different.

This is what I know now: actions and words, however small they may be, mean something. And whatever situation you may be in, filling a person up is so much better than tearing her down.

I remember back then thinking, *It's so hard to know the right thing to do.* There were so many people telling me how I needed to act, who I needed to be, what I needed to say and do, that I felt like I was navigating a minefield. The funny thing is, though, looking back, the "right" path was simple.

Sometimes it takes bravery. Sometimes it takes going against the tide. But kindness is never, ever the wrong choice. And may you never be made to feel guilty or embarrassed for the little slivers of purple paper you send along the way.

# The Sound of Silence

## BASED ON A TRUE STORY
## BY CLAUDIA GABEL

From behind, you'd swear Frances Doyle is a boy. Baggy
pants that hang low off her straight hips. Button-down shirt
with sleeves rolled up to the elbows. Short blond hair that
gets trimmed with an electric razor at the barber shop every
other Tuesday. But from the front, there is no mistaking it—
Frances Doyle is most certainly a girl. Pink, pouty lips and
long, full eyelashes that make all the senior queen bees jealous. Perfectly perky 34Cs, which belong in the pages of the
Victoria's Secret catalog. Small but delicate ears that are
pierced from the lobe all the way up to the cartilage at the
top. If only she'd wear a dress or high-heeled boots or a tight
V-neck sweater to school, things would be a whole lot easier.

But Frances never does and it's pretty obvious why. Although I can't say for sure, because she and I have never really spoken before. Actually, I don't think I've ever heard her say anything to anyone. Not to answer a question in history class or to make a joke to one of her friends at the lunch table. And not a single word to the pack of grade-A butt holes that are tailing her through the hallway right now.

"Hey, dyke!" Bruce Mitchell shouts, his voice just as loud as when he calls plays on the football field.

Frances keeps her head down, eyes locked on the tiles in the floor.

It's Ted Hall's turn to peg her now. He has been copying Bruce's every move since the first grade. "Stop ignoring us, lesbo! We want to talk to you."

I stand by my locker and hold my books close to my chest, watching the spectacle and swallowing hard. This happens every day with each change of class. The flurry of students in the hall acts as camouflage. Sometimes I feel like I'm the only one seeing what I'm seeing. But then I glance over at snotty Hannah Prince and her group of megabitches. They are doing that trademark teenage girl whisper-giggle thing as Frances and her tormentors walk by. So I'm definitely not alone in the audience.

Frances stops at her locker, hands shaking as she attempts to remember its combination while Bruce and company swarm her like angry bees.

"So, Frances, eat anything juicy lately?" Taylor Wells gets within an inch of her face and wags his tongue around.

I think I just threw up in my mouth a little.

The goons laugh. Not one of them tells Taylor to let her be. Suddenly, I am very grateful that none of the boys at this school has ever expressed any interest in me.

Bruce slaps her hard on the shoulder, like she's just one of the guys. "Come on, you can tell us. We're your best friends!"

My heart feels like it is being drilled by the beak of a woodpecker. I pray for the next bell to sound. That will scatter Bruce and his friends like a horde of roaches. I doubt any of them want to get written up. They're always in trouble for something, but never for this. I don't think Frances has ever turned them in. She must believe what everyone else does—tattling on these losers will make the target on your back ten times bigger.

Frances opens her locker and grabs a spiral-bound note-book. I can't help but notice the display of photos on the inside of the door—pictures of Frances with her arm draped over another girl, both of them smiling radiantly. They act-ually kind of look alike. And from the grins on their faces, you can tell they're really happy.

What's so freaking wrong with that?

When Frances shuts the locker and turns around, Ted slaps the notebook out of her grasp, amusing the chuckle-heads that surround him. My skin feels white-hot as I watch

Frances reach for the notebook and hear Taylor cackling while he kicks it down the hall. The notebook lands at the tips of my red patent-leather ballet flats. Everyone else keeps moving along as though nothing out of the ordinary is happening. Someone even plants a Converse sneaker on the notebook, tearing out a couple of scribbled-on pages.

Even Frances's homework gets stepped on.

I know what I should do. Take a deep breath and pick up this notebook. Go over to Frances and offer to walk her to class. I don't even have to acknowledge Bruce and his gang of idiots. We can exit this horrible situation gracefully. In fact, our female solidarity may be so awe inspiring that the hearts of these homophobes may grow three times their size, just like in *How the Grinch Stole Christmas*.

Then I feel Frances's glistening, sad eyes on me, and I can't move. I'm not even sure if I'm breathing, that's how still my body is. There's no doubt that she's talking to me for the very first time. She's asking me for help, and I want to. I *really* want to.

But I'm afraid. One hundred percent frozen solid with fear. I'm ashamed to admit this, but I don't want to give anyone a reason to attack me. I'm not as strong as Frances, who shoves past Bruce amid a barrage of insults that would rip through my heart like a fishing knife.

When she steps in front of me, her neck is completely flushed and her lips are tightened into a thin line, like she is stopping herself from screaming. Instead, Frances bends down and retrieves her notebook, then silently stalks off to the bathroom—the only place she can escape the taunting.

Bruce starts fist bumping his pals, but then the bell sounds and cuts their celebration short. They dart off in different directions, still howling with laughter. The hallway is empty, but I'm still a thick block of ice.

*Here's your chance*, I think. I could sneak off to the principal's office without anyone seeing me. Or I could pop into the bathroom and ask Frances if she's okay. I go back and forth in my mind for a long time.

When my legs are finally able to move, they take me directly to Mr. Caldwell's math class. He gives me a tardy slip as I stroll in. I tuck the piece of paper in my jeans pocket and sit down at my desk, quiet as a mouse.

I'm a coward. That's all there is to it.

Scary thing is, I'll have a chance to redeem myself once class is over, and eight more opportunities tomorrow.

And the day after that. And the day after that. And the day after that . . .

# Starship Suburbia

## BY MARYROSE WOOD

I was bullied in middle school (we called it junior high back then). I was never beaten up or threatened, but I was teased quite a bit for a couple of years. It was because I was a mess.

My family lived in a nice middle-class suburb, but we were fakers. There were five of us: one alcoholic, cigar-smoking, compulsive-gambling dad; one stressed-to-the-point-of-insanity mom; and three smart, shell-shocked kids who were trying to stay out of the crossfire.

We were short on funds and meaningful parental supervision. I often went to school in the same clothes for days on end. Laundry and bathing were an issue. The septic tank was full, but we couldn't afford to get it emptied. "Don't flush until you have to!" was the household motto. We were supposed to put all our toilet paper (used, I'm talking about) in the wastebasket.

That other families flushed their toilet paper was a revelation to me. Almost as much of a revelation as the fact that *Star Trek* was in color. We had a black-and-white TV set. When I saw the show at a friend's house, I gazed in wonder at Captain Kirk's mustard-colored polyester shirt and the way it stretched across those impressive, interplanetary pecs.

As for me, I didn't have a pristine Starfleet uniform to slip into every day. Daily showers were not encouraged. Face it, I was unkempt. I probably smelled bad. In elementary school no one cared. In junior high it became a problem. Seventh-grade girls notice these things.

Interestingly, adults rarely did. Once, a neighbor gently suggested to my mom that, at twelve and already stacked, I might need a bra. Mortified, and without stopping to discuss it or check what my size might be, she went and bought one and tossed it at me, still in the bag. Imagine my surprise when I looked inside!

She said I should wear it because the neighbor made a crack about my bouncing baby B cups. I can't even remember how long I made do with that one ill-fitting bra. I didn't dare put it in the wash; I was afraid I wouldn't see it for a month!

Another time, a relative whom we rarely saw discreetly bought me some deodorant. I used it until it ran out.

So, dirty kid in dirty clothes, mouthful of braces, bra

straps chronically slipping down my arms. What would you do if you were a middle school girl? Would you make comments? Mean ones?

You might. Some kids did, most didn't. I was never without at least a couple of friends. Things sorted out as I got older and figured out how to take care of myself. Meanwhile, the family drama shifted from beer and septic tanks to my dad's horrific lung cancer. He was sick throughout my high school years and died shortly after I turned eighteen.

By then I'd found my social niche. The former teasers got older, too, and nicer. We all ended up friends, more or less. To this day, doing laundry is my favorite household chore.

The kids who teased were wrong to be mean, and it hurt a lot at the time. But, you know, at least they noticed something was wrong.

I kind of wish the grown-ups had, too.

# Kicking Stones at the Sun

## BY JO KNOWLES

When we were kids, my brother, sister, and I took the bus to school every morning. We lived in a rural area and didn't have one of those cool-seeming bus stops where a bunch of kids from the neighborhood gather and wait together at some selected spot. We waited alone at the end of our driveway. In the early years, my brother, who was five years older than me, would ham it up while we waited. He'd go out in the middle of the road and adjust his feet just so on the double yellow lines. We lived at the top of a hill and he'd get down into a tuck position and say he was about to make history skiing on the longest skis in the world. My sister and I would jump on and ski behind him.

When we got a little older, I remember following his lead as he'd look up at our house to make sure our mother wasn't peeking out the window, and then stuff the winter hat she made him wear into the mailbox. I stuffed mine in, too, because if he was too cool to wear a hat, I wanted to be as well. When we got off the bus that afternoon, we'd grab our hats and saunter up the driveway like the angels we never were.

And then in the days just before my brother stopped riding the bus, before he saved money for his own car, I remember how he used to kick pebbles across the road and into the field on the other side. The sun would be coming up in late fall (our bus picked us up at the ungodly hour of 7:00 a.m.), and when I picture him there now, I imagine him kicking stones at the sun with all the grace and rage of a beautiful boy caught in a world that wasn't ready for him.

These are the things I want to remember about my brother. His joy. His skill. His coolness. I loved him so. But I also remember getting on the bus, almost always in the same order. Me first, then my sister, then my brother. I'd sit up front, my sister in the middle, and my brother, bravely, day after day, way in the back.

From my seat behind the driver I could look up into the big mirror she used to supposedly keep her eye on things and see my sister busily talking to her friend, and farther back, my brother. I can see his dirty-blond hair. I can see his face, turning bright red. I can see his eyes, watering. I can see the boys sitting behind him, leaning into his face, saying words that penetrated his heart in some permanent way that shaped him and changed his course for years to come. I see them smash his head against the window. And I see the bus driver, staring straight ahead, humming to the radio.

And then the names.

*Faggot.*

*You little faggot.*

*Sicko.*

These images and words have stayed with me all my life. They have stayed with me just like the other stories my brother told me much later. About how his fourth-grade teacher used to torment him because he was new. From away. But mostly because he was different. We would joke about how Mr. L. had gaydar and what that *really* meant. But we knew it wasn't actually that funny. He told me about how his eleventh-grade teacher said he should just quit school because he would never amount to anything. How he took him out in the hallway during history and slammed him up against the locker, called him a loser. And how, when he and his two best friends went to the principal to report the teacher, the principal didn't believe them.

I was twelve when the real fighting started. I remember the screaming and the crying as my parents pleaded with him not to smoke. Not to drink. Not to do drugs. Not to stay out late. Not to go there or there or there. Not to leave. I remember the pain on his face as he struggled to explain how desperate he was to get out and be with the people who accepted him. I see the agony. The frustration. He just wanted to be loved. To be understood. But he didn't have the words to explain it all. And my parents didn't know how else to protect him. And so he ran away.

The words we hear about ourselves as children are the words we believe until we grow up to know better. I think back now and wonder how different things might have been if just one person with authority had stood up and said "Stop." Or "No." If we'd lived in a time when different was cool. When gay was okay.

But we didn't. And so kids like my brother were on their own. Even the people who loved him so desperately felt helpless. The words he'd heard all through his childhood had been planted so deeply, it would take years to shed them.

We can't do this anymore. We can't pretend that words are just words. We can't say kids will be kids. We can't dismiss cruelty as a rite of passage. We can't be onlookers. We can't say, "I didn't have anything to do with it." We can't teach our kids to not step forward and say "Stop." And "No." We have to say it. We have to shout it.

School administrators can't say it's up to the parents. Parents can't say it's up to the teachers. Teachers can't say it's not their job. And kids can't say, "I was too afraid to tell." Every single one of us has to play our role if we're serious about putting an end to the madness. We are all responsible. We must be.

*Stop.*

*No.*

They are simple words. And they can save lives.

# Memory Videos

## BY NANCY GARDEN

Memory videos play in my mind whenever I hear another child has been bullied.

TAKE ONE:

I'm seven years old, walking home from school in Crestwood, New York. I'm walking carefully because I'm not sure where James is, and I'm afraid of him. He's bigger and older and stronger than I, and every time he goes after me, he wins. This time, though, I'm not as afraid as usual because Daddy has taught me to box so I can fight James.

Suddenly, just as I reach the big hill that goes down to our neighborhood, James darts out from behind a bush and attacks me, punching hard. I make fists and remember which hand guards and which punches—but before I can protect myself or swing, James grabs my arms and pins them behind me, and I burst into tears.

Another time, James and I fight about a dog book while our dogs and my friends watch. Suddenly James ends up facedown on the ground—perhaps my friends have pushed him. His pants slip, and my friends giggle and laugh, pointing to his exposed brown buttocks, speckled with white spots.

James is African-American and the rest of us are white. He's the only black child in my class and probably in the school.

Now that I'm older, I wonder if James became a bully because he'd been bullied himself. That seems likely, and I remember, too, that sometimes he threw up in class after lunch. After the first or second time, the teacher said to us, "When James throws up, I want all of you to get up and leave the room." She showed him no sympathy and was clearly not going to let any of us show him sympathy either.

*Many bullied kids become bullies themselves. Some bullies even become adult criminals.*

I was sorry for James when he threw up, but I didn't do anything about it. Did I laugh with my friends when I saw James's buttocks? My memory video doesn't show me that. But it does show me that I didn't say "Stop!" or "Don't laugh!" or "Let him up!"

I'd gone from being a victim to being a bystander.

*Bystanders who do nothing give bullies permission inadvert-*
*ently to go on being bullies. Most are afraid they'll lose friends*
*or be bullied themselves if they help victims or report bullies,*
*and some feel guilty for years afterward.*

TAKE TWO:

My mother, whose parents and older siblings were born
in Germany, is telling me a story. She's comforting me because
a girl has told me no one likes me because I smile too much.
Worse, two boys have been chasing and attacking me. Kids
have been calling me "four eyes," too. Mum says, "When
I was a Girl Scout during World War One, other children
yelled 'German Spy!' at me as I walked to and from school
in my uniform."

Today I have no idea what prompted the name-calling
or what was the reason for my unpopularity. But the
boys who chased me were children of recent immigrants;
had they been bullied, too, like James, for being "different," "other," "foreign"? My video doesn't tell me that, but I
think Mum was trying to explain that many children are
bullied—not just me.

And of course she was right.

*At the August 2010 government summit about planning a*
*national antibullying strategy, US Secretary of Education Arne*

*Duncan said that every year, 8.2 million kids are bullied at school. He also said that in 2007, more than 900,000 kids in secondary schools reported they'd been cyberbullied (bullied online).*

*In 1995, the National Education Association estimated that every day, 160,000 kids stay home from school because they're afraid they'll be bullied. And at 2010's summit, Duncan said, "A school where children don't feel safe is a school where children struggle to learn. It's a school where kids drop out, tune out, and get depressed."*

*Kids still stay home from school—or give up on school entirely—because they're afraid of being bullied.*

TAKE THREE:

I am grown up. At a political meeting in my hometown, I mention that bullying often occurs on our school buses. "Oh," says one man, "but all kids are bullied—I was bullied." He sounds like the many people who think bullying is a natural part of childhood—a normal rite of passage.

*In 2008, the Yale School of Medicine found that there seems to be a definite connection between being bullied and committing suicide. Would the grieving parents of Phoebe Prince and Carl Joseph Walker-Hoove, both from Massachusetts; Eric Mohat from Ohio; Megan Meier from Missouri; and Ryan Halligan from Vermont—all suicide victims because of being bullied—agree that being bullied is a normal rite of passage?*

More videos race through my head.

TAKE FOUR:

I'm a student teacher, and in the class to which I'm assigned there's a girl who is obviously a lesbian and who I'm sure has been bullied. One day I hear that she's been raped in the girls' bathroom with a Coke bottle by some of her classmates.

*Studies have shown that more than 33 percent of gay, lesbian, and transgender kids are harassed physically in school because of their sexual orientation, and more than 25 percent are harassed because of their gender expression. A study done recently at Nationwide Children's Hospital found that gay, lesbian, and bisexual teens are bullied two to three times more than straight ones.*

TAKE FIVE:

I can see this video clearly, because the boy it's about is someone my partner and I helped bring up. Let's call him Kevin. Kevin's slight of build, has a pleasant, friendly face and a neat sense of humor, and his light brown hair tends to drape over his forehead. He's the closest thing to a son I've ever had.

Now picture a sprawling one-story high school building with a flat roof. Put Kevin on top of it with other boys around him—and watch as the other boys hang him by his heels from the roof.

Thank God he neither fell nor later, like Phoebe Prince, Carl Joseph Walker-Hoover, and many others, committed suicide.

But years later, after Columbine, Kevin told me and my partner that had it not been for music, basketball, and people like us to talk with, he might well have taken a gun to school and used it, like Eric Harris and Dylan Klebold at Columbine High.

*In 2002, research done by the Secret Service and the US Department of Education found that 75 percent of the school shooters they studied were victims of bullying.*

There are thousands of bullying incidents every day.

Bullies and bystanders are caught in a cruel vortex of aggression and fear.

Every single bullying victim hurts.

Some kill themselves.

Those who survive bear hidden scars forever.

# Finding Light in the Darkness
## BY LISA SCHROEDER

*In the darkness of the night,*
*I shiver under the covers,*
*unable to free myself*
*from the bitter cold*
*hidden in the disgust you shove at me.*

*In the darkness of the hallway,*
*I spill invisible blood,*
*unable to protect myself*
*from the sharp sting*
*of the insults you throw at me.*

*In the darkness of the streets,*
*I cower as you come at me,*
*unable to defend myself*

*from the very real terror*
*behind the threats you kick at me.*

*In the darkness*
*I cry.*

*In the darkness*
*I wish.*

*In the darkness*
*I pray.*

*In the light of my family room,*
*I tell her of the coldness,*
*able to see*
*it's not me*
*who is weak.*

*In the light of an office,*
*I tell him of the pain,*
*able to see*
*it's not me*
*who is ignorant.*

*In the light of a new day,*
*we stand side by side*
*and we tell the world*

*we must not tolerate hatred,*
*able to see*
*it is us*
*who will bring change.*

# WRITE IT

# The Sandwich Fight

## BY STEVEN E. WEDEL

The noise of the lunchroom was loud, rising and falling as the lower grades of Coolidge Elementary talked and ate, ignoring the illuminated red of the traffic light that indicated it was quiet time. Being a picky eater, I'd opted to bring my lunch. I took my sandwich—thin sheets of beef lunch meat with mustard on white bread—from my Charlie Brown lunch box and brought it toward my mouth.

"Give me a bite." The voice belonged to Kevin. Something inside me squirmed, looking for a deeper place to hide.

A few days earlier, Kevin had demanded one of my mom's homemade chocolate chip cookies. I refused. He stole one. When I complained to my mom, her response was that I should have shared my cookies. Now, I'm not opposed to sharing. Never have been. But it goes all over me when somebody demands I give up something that is mine. Kevin had stolen my cookie, and now he was sitting there in his yellow button-down shirt, his own lunch in front of him, insisting I give him a bite of my sandwich.

There was more to it, of course. This was second grade, 1972, and only the first year for Enid, Oklahoma, schools to have a hot lunch program. I tried a hot lunch the second day of school and hated it, so I took my lunch every day from then on. Looking back, I suppose it was fitting I carried a Charlie Brown lunch box, considering how much ol' Chuck and I had in common. Something inside made us easy targets for harassment. Charlie Brown had his Lucy, and I had Kevin.

Earlier in the year, he'd stolen my eraser. Our teacher, Mrs. Patton, was leading a group of kids in reading while I was whispering to Kevin to give back my eraser. The girl next to me was trying to help resolve the issue. Next thing I knew, Mrs. Patton was swatting Kevin, then the girl, and then had me by the ear and was dragging me out of my desk and lighting up my butt with her wooden paddle. Hey, it was the early seventies and that stuff was still allowed.

Classroom, playground, he was always there, always picking on me about something. But nowhere was it worse than the lunchroom.

I lifted the thin sandwich toward my mouth for a second bite, and he grabbed my wrist. We struggled, him pulling my hand and food toward his open mouth. How long until a teacher noticed? Would I get in trouble for this, too? Another swat?

He got his bite. No way I was eating that after his mouth had touched it. I dropped it back into my lunch box and ate whatever else Mom had packed. But it wasn't over. He loved the idea that I wouldn't eat the sandwich now and amped up the harassment until, finally, I agreed to settle the matter with him on the playground after school.

The rest of the day was horrible. I was a bundle of nerves. We'd get caught. That was certain. I'd get in trouble at school. They'd call home. Mom would be mad. Dad would be mad. I'd probably get spanked and grounded and Dad— my Pentecostal father—would give me a lecture about turning the other cheek while my mom would settle the issue by making an extra sandwich or cutting mine in half so I could share it.

There were ways out, of course. I could tell on Kevin. However, Mrs. Patton didn't approve of that. In fact, she usually pinned a long strip of paper to the butt of anyone who told on classmates; she encouraged and led the way in calling people tattletales. No joke. This is the same teacher who told the class's only black student that he'd melt into a puddle of chocolate if he didn't stop sweating in class. Remember, early seventies.

I could try to leave through a different door, but Kevin would most likely just follow me. I could pretend to be sick and go home early, but Mom would know I wasn't sick and

I'd get in trouble for that and probably have to explain why I really went home.

Not fighting was an option . . . but was it a good one? What was in store for me if I didn't go through with the fight? There would be more bullies in later grades. Oh, and junior high. Is there a worse time in anybody's life? Puberty lay in wait for me, and it had nasty plans. My face would become a constant mass of red, oozing acne. Blackheads, whiteheads, the works. I'd hit a growth spurt in which I seemed to grow taller by a few inches every month or so, making my jeans always too short and my shirts too tight.

Not standing up now would keep me from fighting back if some punk who used to be my friend dragged me out of the boys' restroom while I was changing out of my band uniform, casting me to the hallway floor in just a shirt, socks, and my tighty-whities, right in front of some preppy girls. Avoiding Kevin now would mean I'd do nothing when clubbed over the head at my locker or when my face was slammed against another guy's crotch.

If I didn't fight, how would I handle the mob of boys waiting to torment me in ninth grade because I chose a girl-friend who was a year younger than me? How would I deal with the name-calling, the punch-and-runs in the hall, the tripping, and everything else?

I think both second-grade classes turned out for the fight. Word gets around. There were a lot of kids out there.

They made a ring around me and Kevin on the playground behind the school. They were bloodthirsty in their plaid bell-bottoms and cotton dresses.

Oddly, I wasn't so much worried about losing the fight. I'd never been in a fight before. I wasn't even sure how it was supposed to work. My only fear was of getting caught.

It was time. Kevin and I closed in on each other. We locked arms in some kiddie wrestling move and held for a few seconds before breaking free.

I ran. I snatched my Charlie Brown lunch box and books off the sidewalk and ran all the way home.

The next several years were off-and-on hell as I dealt with one bully after another, always too timid to stand up for myself. Eventually I grew out of being the scrawny, acne-riddled kid in clothes that didn't fit. Sometime after that, most of my bullies matured, but by that time I'd learned that I had to stand up to them, even if it meant a fight. Even if it meant losing the fight. Even if it meant getting in trouble for fighting.

I believe everything that happens to us goes into making us what we are. We are a collection of our experiences. Yeah, I suffered a lot of abuse because I chose to run away from that fight, but in the end I think everything I endured made me a better person and better teacher and certainly gave me a lot of material to write about.

# Fearless

## BY JEANNINE GARSEE

At thirteen, I'm smart, mouthy, and fearless.

Overnight, I change.

Our junior high is a battlefield, the enemy line clearly drawn: me on one side, along with Dee-Dee and Diane, and *them*—Renee, Cathy, and Judith—on the other. We six spend our days trading sinister stares, snide remarks, and bumps in the hall. It's not a popularity issue; we're all equally unpopular. Not jealousy, either; as daughters of working class families, our wardrobes aren't special, plus we're *all* plagued with acne, bad hair, and iffy figures. No cheerleaders, no jocks, no honor roll members among us—just six average, awkward eighth-grade girls.

We simply hate one another. Without a huge circle of friends of our own, and linked by our mutual contempt for *them*, Dee-Dee, Diane, and I vow to always stick together.

One evening, a classmate I know casually calls to say, "I heard some people are out to get you."

"What? *Who?*"

"I can't say. But I thought I'd warn you." *Click.*

Wondering if Dee-Dee or Diane know about this, I phone Dee-Dee first—*and she hangs up on me!* Baffled and uneasy, I then try Diane.

"People don't like you anymore," she admits after a long silence.

"People? What people?"

"*Everyone.*" Then Diane hangs up, too.

Sick with dread, I agonize over this all night long. In the morning, as usual, I wait for Dee-Dee's mom, who generally drives the three of us to school. The clock ticks away. No one shows up. Nauseated, wondering what I'll be walking into today, I rush to school on foot, barely making it on time.

When I stumble into Mrs. Z.'s homeroom, Dee-Dee glares. Diane averts her eyes. I mumble "Hi" anyway, but they both ignore me. Seated, I peek nervously around—and make a hideous discovery.

It's not only Dee-Dee and Diane who are in on this game; *everyone's* battering me with nasty looks! They whisper. They toss notes back and forth and then point purposefully to me. When Mrs. Z. calls my name, someone shouts "Horseface!" and the entire class screeches with laughter.

"Enough of that!" Mrs. Z. snaps, which only prompts a quieter litany of "*Horseface . . . Horseface . . .*" She pretends not to hear them.

So do I.

Shaky, sweaty, my stomach burning, I rack my brain to figure this all out: *Why is this happening? What did I do to Dee-Dee and Diane? We were fine yesterday!*

The day straggles on, each class a rerun of the one before. People call me names, throw spitballs at me. At lunch, when I spot Dee-Dee and Diane *chatting* with Renee, Cathy, and Judith, my situation becomes horrifyingly clear.

Yes, my two best friends have joined ranks with *them.*

Sickened by this blatant betrayal, I sit far away, yet not nearly far enough; I can still hear their comments about "what a bitch she is" and how they hope to "kick her ass!" When a balled-up lunch bag smacks me in the head, I ditch my uneaten lunch and slink off to the library.

After school, when nobody kicks my ass, I walk home alone, praying for a miracle. *Make tomorrow different. Make things normal again. Make it all a bad joke. Please, God, please!*

But the next day, nothing has changed. Attempts by teachers to stop the harassment have little effect; what my new enemies can't accomplish in class, they take to the halls. They snatch my books, push me and trip me, spit in my face, and jerk my hair. They call me "Horseface" incessantly.

They tell lies, spread rumors.

And this lasts . . .

. . . and lasts.

Day after day.

Week after week.

One endless, unimaginable nightmare.

When Dee-Dee and Diane rebuff my timid attempts to make up—*for what? What? I don't even know!*—I lapse into a numbing depression. I sleep as much possible, hoping I won't wake up. On better days, I plot my revenge, fantasizing gory events I know I'll never carry out. I frequently play sick, missing days of school on end. The only advice my distant parents have to offer is "If you ignore them, they'll leave you alone." They are so, so wrong.

Ostracized and alone, I'm sure of only one thing: People hate me.

*Hate me!*

And though I hate them back, I know I'll forgive them in an instant—if only they'll forgive *me* for whatever I did to them.

I try one last time and telephone Diane. "*Please* tell me why everyone hates me!"

"You're too tough," she says flatly. "You're a tomboy."

For *that* my so-called friends turned the whole class against me? I plead for more details. She merely hangs up on me.

Regardless of Diane's words, I know I've *lost* all my

toughness. I feel trapped and helpless, irreparably broken. *I'll never survive the rest of the year*, I think. *Something will happen to me first . . . something terrible!*

I do survive, and it's my writing that saves me. Not only do I detail this experience in my diary, but I also plunge into writing fiction to escape my reality. I spend my lunch periods in the library plotting out new worlds. I huddle over my typewriter long past midnight, inventing characters less cowardly than me, ones with far happier lives.

Eighth grade ends at last. Ninth grade turns out to be nearly as insufferable. By sophomore year, the abuse dwindles, though I occasionally hear "Horseface!" directed at me in the halls. After two years, Dee-Dee, shyly, attempts to renew our old friendship. I'm polite but superficial; I don't *care* about her anymore. Nor can I forgive her.

Writing now with a feverish vengeance, I finish my first novel by the end of tenth grade: the story of a girl who is smart, mouthy, and fearless.

*I am me. I am whole.*

No one can break me again.

# Without Armor

## BY DANIEL WATERS

"You're the guy who writes about dead kids," she said, her mouth tight. It wasn't a statement or a question; it was an accusation.

I'll admit the comment threw me. Obviously, I'd never been on a book tour before, much less a prepublication tour, and had little idea of what to expect. To be more accurate, I'd tried to keep myself free from expectations. Doing so allowed me to enjoy the process much more than if I had obsessed over everything like I usually do.

The downside of walking around open to the world, free from expectation, is that it involves taking one's armor off. All writers have armor. Armor is required gear for anyone who willfully engages in a career path fraught with rejection, public criticism, or, worse, obscurity. I actually think my armor is pretty tough, battle hardened by far too many years trying and failing to "break in." But like any other writer's, it is patchy and cobbled together out of spare parts, rife with weak spots that could let deadly, near-mortal wounds pass through. Regardless, I'd left it home.

You'd think after writing a book about dead kids, and dead kids falling in love with living kids and vice versa, that I'd have been a little more battle ready. I may officially be an author of young adult books, but I'd grown up thinking I would be a horror author, and so I read all the introductions to great horror novels and anthologies. These were usually autobiographical in nature, and almost invariably the intros had some anecdote about the social awkwardness of being a horror author. I gathered that it was weird enough being a "normal" author (World to author: What is it you really do?), but horror authors, it seemed, dealt with another level of bizarre social awkwardness entirely. Some of their experiences I read about included having their books banned, getting ostracized by the local PTA at their children's schools, being accosted constantly by armchair psychoanalysts, or— one of my favorites—fielding questions like "Ever et raw meat?" (one posed to Mr. Stephen King, who has many such anecdotes). A horror author clearly had to deal with a segment of the public that was less than adoring and, in many cases, downright hostile. Maybe I should have done more to guard myself against such hostility.

There was a pause as I took note of the woman's posture,

her tone, the glint in her eyes. She wanted to fight. Did I? Am I the guy who writes about dead kids? A hundred responses, mostly defensive, many belligerent, sprang to my mind. Responses about judging books by covers and did you actually read the book or do you actually read any books and much, much worse. As a writer, you don't get to tell someone the meaning of what they just read. That's the job of the book itself. You can, however, talk about what informed the writing, what your mood was, and what was going on in your head when you were writing the story.

The initial idea for *Generation Dead* came from some newsmagazine show I'd seen on violence in schools. According to the program, it was becoming all the rage in schools across America to videotape planned fights or random acts of violence and put them up on YouTube for the entire world to enjoy. The show ran a number of the actual clips of young people hurting other young people. One of the clips featured a little boy in a coat that was too big for him waiting for the bus to arrive. A much larger boy ran into the frame and punched the smaller boy in the face, dropping him to the pavement. The little boy sat, alone and crying, bleeding from his nose and mouth.

We've all got our horror pressure points. That was mine. That's what I wrote about.

Well, really I wrote a love story. That's what it says on the dedication page, anyway: *For Kim, a love story.* The back cover copy of the book promises love and romance and those topics are what, presumably, the marketing efforts will highlight. And if you ask me, I will tell you I wrote a love story. It just happens to be a love story with zombies. Teenage zombies.

But the damaged boy crying on the pavement is in the book, too, as are the damaged boys that attacked and filmed him. You won't see them as you see Tommy, the living-impaired boy who falls for Phoebe, the traditionally biotic girl who notices that Tommy is different from all the other boys in her class in more ways than the obvious one. The YouTube victim and his assailants aren't physical characters in the book, but they are there lurking somewhere under the surface of the story.

I think the zombies were my brain's (my braaaaaiiiiiin's!) way of coping with what to me was a truly horrific subject. Cthulhu scares me. Dracula is creepy, and I fear the Rough Beast slouching toward Bethlehem, but the idea (no, not the idea, the reality) of a kid injuring another kid for no other reason than the entertainment value he assumes to be inherent in the act absolutely horrifies me. The zombies allowed me to inject humor into a subject matter that, if I dwelled on it for too long, would put me in the deepest blue funk imaginable. The zombies helped me cope.

And zombies are, of course, wicked cool.

I wrote a story that thrilled me and gripped me emotionally. *Generation Dead* made me laugh, it made me sad, and it scared me. Writing about love and death and zombies and being young and never growing old taught me so much. I wrote about things that were important to me, and while I may not have known what I was trying to do when I started, by the time I finished I had a very clear sense of what I'd written and what I was trying to do as a writer. And I care very deeply about those kids—the kids on YouTube and the kids in my book. My dead kids are not "dead kids" in the sense that the tight-lipped woman was implying.

Which brings us back to Danny's First Critic. She taught me something. She taught me that I'm better off without the armor, because no matter how much I fortify it, no matter how well oiled the plates are, and no matter how tightly I weave the chain links, there's no way it can really protect me. An arrow can always slip through; a swung club could always bruise. And that's okay, really, because it is as much a part of my job to feel as it is to make others feel.

I'm glad I'd left the armor at home. If I'd prepared for battle, I don't think I would have answered her in quite the same way, and I don't think my answer, in turn, would have made her grim expression soften. I don't think she would have done what she did next, which was pick up the advanced reader copy of the book and add it to the considerable pile she had already amassed. She didn't go as far as to have me sign it, but she took the book.

"No," I'd told her, "I'm the guy who writes about kids who're trying to live."

293

# The Seed

## BY LAUREN KATE

There is a girl in your seventh-grade class. She is not exceptionally pretty. She isn't rich or all that great of a singer. She is no more or less popular than you. You are friends with each other's friends, but you are not friends.

There are meaner girls than this one. Your school is teeming with them. Down every hallway lurk bigger snobs and scarier gossips. And yet, for some reason, ever since your elementary school and this girl's elementary school flowed together into one great big middle school, this is the girl who makes you feel the most uncomfortable in your skin.

In the mornings, she and her friends stand outside the cul-de-sac where the bus drops off, handing out religious pamphlets. When you don't take one—and you never take one—she is the girl who always asks, loudly enough for the whole bus full of kids to hear, why you want to burn in hell for all eternity. This is the worst, but not the last, of it. In gym, she flirts with the boys you have crushes on. In English, your favorite class, she challenges the things you say about the reading assignment to the point where you are dumbstruck, even though you know the answer. On the rare occasions when you and your friends are being mean girls—once, at a slumber party, after the first girl fell asleep, you and your friends soaked her extra underwear and put it in the freezer—this girl rolls over in her sleeping bag and catches you, singles you out, makes you feel worse than your own mother did when she heard about the incident.

This girl may not even know it, but she has perfected the art of making you feel as if everything you do, everything you say, and especially everything you *don't* say is under her scrutiny, and wrong.

You are not good at comebacks. This isn't something that will ever change, by the way, even twenty years down the road. The words that were *nowhere near* the tip of your tongue at the critical moment begin to haunt you. They keep you up at night. You lie in bed, replaying the dialogue that left you speechless earlier that day. The way this girl kept pressing you to talk about why you weren't going to the school dance—in front of the boy you wish had asked you.

Here's the difference: In your mind, you're wearing cooler clothes. You visualize every detail, down to the way your socks are scrunched (this is Texas, after all). Your cheeks don't turn bright red and your voice doesn't shake and you don't spit out a lame and unconvincing excuse about your grandparents coming into town. In your mind, you say something funny, really funny, that makes the boy who was pretending not to hear your conversation laugh out loud. Also, it shuts the girl up. For a change.

The fantasy of a perfect conversation becomes a nightly ritual. You don't know it yet, but this is the beginning of your career as a writer. And this girl—the one you cannot stand—planted the seed in you. In your imagination, you are the smartest, funniest version of yourself. You are inventing the person you want to practice being, and she's brilliant. So brilliant someone should write a book about her.

You grow up a little bit. Some things change and some don't. The girl stops handing out those little blue copies of the New Testament, but she still makes you tongue-tied most of the time. At least the cute boy from gym class doesn't do that anymore. It's easy to say the thing that makes him laugh. Another dance is coming up. You have a date.

Years later, you leave home. In college, you meet people who remind you of this girl. The difference is you don't let them get under your skin. All those nights, all those scenes you played out in your head—it's as if they have given you wings. You've even started writing a few of them down. Before you know it, you've written a book. You call it *The Betrayal of Natalie Hargrove*.

IT GETS BETTER

# Now

## BY AMY REED

No.

Look.

I am not the timid little thing you remember. These are not the hallways that you owned. This is not the place where things worked backward, where feral children ruled the world.

You remember the girl who played possum. She went limp and you knew how to bend her, your puppet, your perfect soft thing. But maybe one day her muscles tensed. She opened her eyes and she saw you trying to hide in the shadows. But it was day, and you were exposed. It was day, and light favors goodness. She could see through the place where a heart should have been. She could see through you, and those veils and mirrors you thought indestructible ripped and shattered into a million pieces.

You remember. This was the day she stopped playing dead.

Was this it? Was this the thing that broke you, the insult that turned you rabid? Was she too much life for you to smother?

You tried. The way something rabid tries.

Now.

There are years and miles and heartbeats between us. There is a big, beautiful world and you are not in it. You live in a small place, and it is not here. It is the only place that will take you—locked away, dark. You are fighting the walls, thrashing around and trying to gain power. But you are the small one now. You are the tiny speck of a thing. You are a ghost, and ghosts are not solid. They are not flesh, not a thing that breathes, not my heart beating.

This is.

Take a good look at my life now, my heart beating. This is the world I have built and it is my own. This breath, this blood, this music—all mine. This is how things grow, how they reach toward the sun. You can have that little speck of yesterday, the place where ghosts roam, that broken, rotten thing. I do not need it anymore. There is tomorrow, and another tomorrow after that. There is today, and it is not yours.

Now.

Look at everything around me so solid. This is light, my beautiful thing. These are my hands and here are the things they touch. This is what gentle looks like. These are my eyes, wide and trusting. Look, my hands are not fists. They are open. This is what brave looks like.

Yes.

There are people with hearts all around me. Not holes. Not empty places to see through. Yes. Solid. I am reaching for them and they are reaching, too. Look. Light. This is love and it is stronger than you.

# Standing Tall

## BY DAWN METCALF

It started in kindergarten.

I was tall. Taller than all the kids in my class, taller than most kids in the next grade; in a few years, I'd be taller than my teachers, but at five years old, I was long haired, shy, gangly, and, above all, tall.

There was a boy who was not tall. Let's call him Dickie. Dickie was the smallest boy in our class and I was the tallest girl. That was all it took.

Dickie would torment me. He'd hit me with blocks. He'd poke me with pencils. He'd call me names I didn't understand and when I'd tattle to the teacher, she'd tell me to sit down. I had made one or two new friends when I'd transferred to this new school, but most often I'd sit by myself on the edge of the blacktop during recess and read a book. Dickie, however, would not leave me alone. He led a group of boys and girls. He'd dare them to tag me as they ran by or surround my spot by the crab apple tree and call me nasty names. I'd try to ignore them, tightening my arms and legs and keeping an eye on my book as the words started to swim. When I'd had enough, I'd stand up all of a sudden and the kids would scatter, squealing. I remember the look on Dickie's face—he was joyously terrified.

Then I'd sit down and go back to reading.

Later, I'd run home crying.

This pattern continued throughout elementary and middle school. The name-calling became smoother, delivered with a sneer. The poking with pencils graduated to elbowing. The taggish slaps became a snatch to snap a bra strap that wasn't even there—it set the tone for my days at school: Middle School Hell.

Now I was taller than the principal, wearing glasses and braces and there was nowhere to hide.

I no longer cried. I was tired and hated school and would fantasize loudly to all my friends about how my family was going to move and I was going to get out of this stupid town before the end of the year. (When my father didn't accept the offer to move to Seattle, I was crushed.) I had to face it: I was stuck until high school graduation—thirteen years of Dickie.

I was eleven years old and five foot eight. I joined the basketball team. My job was to stand in the middle of the court with my arms raised, preventing most kids from even seeing the net. I was a wall, which pretty much describes my entire middle school experience: I stood there and I took it. Day after day. Year after year. But secretly I wanted—just once—to set aside my parents' hippie values of Love and Peace and Togetherness on Earth and grab any of these yappy little dogs by the scruffs of their necks and . . . but that wasn't very Zen. Instead, I swallowed it down and wrote novels at home.

I entered high school at five nine and age fourteen and it was heaven because it was *tall*. It was the eighties, a loud, colorful time of big hair and high-heeled boots, and I didn't feel anything out of the ordinary anymore because I learned something new in high school: sarcasm was street cred. Innuendo was my shield and dry wit my sword. Add my family's patented humor and I soon had a group of friends who didn't mind that I was taller than them. There were even two guys, Jay and Marcus, who were *taller* than me! We could have entire conversations over the heads of our classmates while walking down the hall, although I'd grown used to placing my left foot forward, slumping my shoulders slightly, and tilting my chin down to speak. It never occurred to me to notice how tall someone was (or wasn't) or how heavy they were (or weren't); I think I'd purposefully gone blind to such differences, shaping my eyes to level the playing field. I was surprised by photos that showed my friends were all so much shorter than me. They never seemed that way in real life. We all felt equal.

And if my bullies were in my classes, I didn't notice. I had my own friends, a boyfriend, a chosen profession (writer!), and my own high school drama; I couldn't be bothered much by theirs. The yappy dogs weren't part of my world any longer.

That is, until one day in chemistry class near the end of senior year when Dickie stopped at the front of my row. He leaned over my desk.

"I have a black belt," he said evenly, "in judo."

I honestly had no idea why he was telling me this. Was it a threat? A dare? I said nothing and went back to reading my notes. He walked away, a smug smile on his face, and I let him go.

No, really. In that instant, I let him go.

Maybe I was being a bigger person (pun intended) or secretly withholding my snark or having a sudden case of esprit de l'escalier, but I hadn't said what had instantly popped into my mind, although it made me smile:

"And yet, you're *still* shorter than me."

Thus ended the wrath of Dickie.

Ironically, years later, I married a Shaolin Kempo instructor and I learned something important about the martial arts: if Dickie had been any kind of black belt worth his salt, there would have been no reason to tell me his rank unless he felt that it was in self-defense.

Unless he felt threatened.

By li'l ol' me.

# The Superdork of the Fifth-Grade Class of 1989

## BY KRISTIN HARMEL

It was the end of the eighties. Big hair was in. At Shorecrest School, everybody who was anybody was wearing Z Cavaricci or Esprit.

I, of course, wasn't. In fact, I didn't own a single designer item. This, apparently, made me a complete *nobody*.

At least, that's what the kids at my new school said.

My family had just moved to Florida from Ohio, meaning that I was one of the only new kids in a class that had been together since kindergarten. It also meant that on my first day of fifth grade, when I showed up in my favorite Superman T-shirt and a hot pink skirt, I marked myself as "different," which was apparently entirely unacceptable.

"Like, where are your Z Cavaricci shorts?" asked the girl

sitting beside me in Mrs. Hallinan's homeroom that first morning.

"Z what?" I asked blankly.

"Like, *no way*," she said disdainfully. "You don't even know what that is? Omigod, the new girl is *so lame!*" She turned away, her nose wrinkled in outrage, and whispered something to the girl beside her. Both of them collapsed in giggles.

I'd come from a school where kids still played freeze tag at recess, hadn't had their first kisses yet, and wore jeans and T-shirts from JCPenney and Sears. Suddenly, at this new school, I was a complete outcast due to the fact that my parents didn't drive a BMW or Mercedes, I didn't carry a designer purse, and I hadn't already made it to third base with a boy (heck, I wouldn't even have my first kiss for another four years!).

The remainder of fifth grade was pretty much downhill from there. Aside from a few high points, including a friend-ship with a wonderful girl named Katharine (also a new girl, who had just moved from England), I remember fifth grade by these events:

At the end of week one, I scored a lunch seat at the "pop-ular" table, and when I laughed at popular guy Eric's joke, I wound up spewing out a bright red slushy, through my *nose*, all over him. Any shot I had at being anything but the fifth grade's Superdork was gone at that moment.

Once, while flirting with Matt, the boy I liked, I threatened to "bop him over the head" with my notebook if he didn't stop teasing me. The class's Little Miss Popular, Saria, overheard and shouted to the entire class, "Kristin wants to bop Matt! That means she wants to have sex with him! Bop, bop, bop! Ewww!" I thus became known as the Superdork Who Wants to Have Sex with Matt.

I finalized my outcast status midautumn when Saria stopped by my desk to loudly ask what celebrity I would want to sleep with if I had the chance. "Uh, I don't really want to sleep with *any* celebrities," I stammered. Considering that I was ten and hardly knew what sex was, I don't think that was a particularly odd answer, but to Saria, apparently it was laughably foolish. Within five minutes, the entire class had been informed that I was a "frigid bitch" who'd never have a boyfriend.

Yep, fifth grade was miserable. Led by Saria, the "popular" students tortured me endlessly. They made fun of the nondesigner clothes I wore and told me I dressed like a boy. They laughed at the Oldsmobile station wagon my mother drove, while they roared off with their parents in expensive sports cars. They told me that the cool guys they loved, people like Jon Bon Jovi and Joey McIntyre, would never go for a flat-chested, plain dork like me, so I might as well just die now, because no one important would ever love me anyhow. (It never occurred to me that Bon Jovi and the

New Kids were also rather unlikely to fall madly in love with *any* of the snotty ten-year-olds surrounding me, but I digress.) I went home from school and cried into my pillow a few times a week.

My mom kept telling me it would get better. I didn't believe her. I thought that in Florida, maybe I'd be a geek forever. I'd always be wearing the wrong clothes, thinking the wrong things, and totally missing the boat when it came to boys.

That was around the time I read *Anne Frank: The Diary of a Young Girl.* It was a book that changed my life. I realized that in a way—on a much, much smaller scale—the bullies of the fifth grade were a little like the people who stole the life of that sweet, young, hopeful girl. Like the Nazis, I thought, the bullies didn't think for themselves; they just dressed the way they were supposed to dress, thought the way they were told to think, and tried their best to make life miserable for anyone "different." Anne Frank's situation had been infinitely, unbelievably worse than mine; yet she'd remained hopeful and refused to let them steal her spirit. Maybe, I thought, I should try to do the same.

When I went to a new school for sixth grade, things began to change. I stood up for myself from the start. I didn't let people walk on me. And although I still didn't cloak myself in designer duds, I committed early on to being proud to rock the clothes I wanted to rock. I thought often of Anne Frank's words: "The final forming of a person's character lies in their own hands." Like Anne Frank, I couldn't control the world around me, but I *could* control my own perspective and what went on in my own heart.

By high school, I was still doing things that would have gotten me bullied in fifth grade: I was in the marching band; I was making straight As; and I still dressed in jeans and tees because they were more comfortable than designer dresses and heels. I was still flat-chested; I still hadn't slept with a boy; I still had silly crushes and said silly things.

But here's the difference: By high school, I'd made a decision. I was never going to be the coolest kid in school, nor would I wear the most expensive clothes or date the popular boys. But I was going to be *me*. And instead of letting people make me feel bad about myself, I was going to surround myself only with people who were kind, even if they were outcasts, too. And furthermore, I was going to stand up for people I saw being picked on.

And you know what happened? When I stopped feeling bad about myself and letting the bullies get the best of me, my attitude attracted other kind people. And by my senior year, *we* were the biggest group in the school, and thus the most popular ones. By typical high school standards, the fact that I was both the valedictorian and the drum major of the marching band should have resigned me to total geekdom, right? But in this case, because we'd worked hard to make our school a place where individuality was respected, I was not only *not* a geek but I was also the prom queen.

As my friend Ken is fond of saying, "Kind is the new cool." And it is; that's a secret I discovered back when I was in school, and it's a thought I've lived by ever since.

There are probably always going to be mean kids; I suspect every school has its bullies. But you know what? I tell you from the bottom of my heart that the mean kids will never prosper. They may rule elementary, middle, and high schools around the country, but when they're thrust into *real* adult society, they realize soon enough that cruelty and derision don't pay. Not in the long term.

I've run into a few of the bullies from my childhood in the years since. Without exception, those who were the cruelest when we were kids have done almost nothing with their lives. One is even in jail. They peaked in their teens, and it's been all downhill from there. Most of them are miserable, unfulfilled, and wishing they could go back to their glory days, when they were ten or twelve or sixteen. What kind of life is that?

I, on the other hand, have written six books. I have dozens of friends around the country and, indeed, around the world. I've dated celebrities (Take that, Saria!), seen my dreams come true, traveled to the places I've read about. Fifth grade was miserable, and I was the object of a year full of bullying torture. But now I'm happy, and like Anne

Frank once wrote long ago, "whoever is happy will make others happy, too." I hope that sometimes I'm able to do that in my life. I keep trying.

My life isn't perfect, but it's fulfilling. And most of all, because I try to live my life with kindness, I wake up every morning with a clean conscience and a smile in my heart.

Not bad for the Superdork of Shorecrest's fifth-grade class of 1989.

# "Who Gives the Popular People Power? Who???"

## BY MEGAN McCAFFERTY

I have a survey I filled out at the end of first grade. In it, I ranked myself the smartest, funniest, and most popular girl in my class. This wasn't a case of egotistically inflated self-worth; I was merely documenting the truth. I was the girl other girls wanted to sit next to at lunch, be partners with on school trips, and invite to Friday-night sleepovers. I didn't try hard to be liked. I just was. My likability was effortless in a way that it would never be again.

Because things changed. Drastically.

*January 1*
*My class at school sucks!*

For me, sixth grade was the *worst*. It's no coincidence, then, that it was also the year I discovered the therapeutic powers of writing and began chronicling in my diary all the backstabbing and casual playground cruelty.*

*March 15*
*Amy and I aren't good friends anymore. She's always over Heather's house. Like today I was gonna sleep over her house but she canceled because she's going to the movies with Heather. Amy talks about Heather behind her back all the time (and denies doing it). I really hate this, I really do. I can't compete with Heather. Who gives the popular people power? Who???*

By the time I graduated Bayville Elementary School, I wasn't popular anymore. Not even close. And the worst part about it was that I didn't understand why. I was still the one who got straight As and could do a funny moonwalk on the blacktop, but smarts and a sense of humor weren't valued qualities anymore. The rules for social success had been rewritten, and no one had bothered to send me a copy.

*March 19*
*Right now I'm pretty miserable. When I went outside to play kickball they said the game was locked and I couldn't*

---

* Note: Names have changed, but all other details are taken directly from the original source material.

314

*join. What hurts most is that Amy played on without saying anything. I used to be the only person on her side when Heather got mad at* her. *I was a real friend! I know this is bad but I hope they* all *get mad at her. Then she'd really see who's on her side and her friend. (I know it's mean.) I really don't have a lot of friends now so it's not easy. I seriously think there is not one person who knows how to be a true-blue, one-of-a-kind, till-the-end friend. Geez, maybe I don't even know, but at least I try—honest I do. I just don't see why everyone adores Heather. I am (I don't want to brag or lie) a* lot *nicer than her. Well, before I depress you (and me) I better go.*

It didn't make much sense to me that the most popular girls were the ones who were more feared than admired. No one seemed to like them very much at all. Well, except the boys.

*April 12*
*Everyone got mad at me because they said I said Heather is a* slut. *(She* is *but I didn't say so.) When I walked into math class everyone shoved notes in my face. All of them said things like* Rot in Hell. *Heather said she was going to kick my ass in.*

That was it! I'd solved the mystery! The most popular girls were the ones who were wanted by the boys! The only problem was, I was not one of those girls.

*May 19*
*I wish I was prettier. Nobody likes me. I'm a sad case. That's all I have to say.*

Far worse than not being pretty or popular: I didn't have a single friend I could trust. Just when I thought I had found someone who liked me for who I was, I'd find out that I was dead wrong.

*June 3*
*Today in school Jennifer wrote a note to Heather. While she was reading it, I turned to talk to her and I saw in big print I HATE MEGAN!!! This was the same person who was at my house over the weekend laughing and having a good time with my computer.*

*Why do people have to talk about each other like that? If I don't like someone, I don't hang around her. I hate this entire year in school!*

*I can't really confide in anyone with my deepest feelings. Only you. You won't tell.*

Writing in my diary obviously didn't transform me into the girl the boys wanted to kiss and the other girls wanted to be. It didn't make any of my problems go away. But at least

I had an outlet for my angst, one that would never betray my confidence.

*June 17*
*We got our yearbooks today. When I signed Amy's I put that I hoped to see her over the summer. When she read it she said really sarcastically, "Yeah, I'll come over every day and do the Jersey Devil snort!" Then she walked away laughing. It used to be a joke between us. I can't understand how someone who was my best friend could do that. It really hurt. I hung out with her most of last summer and now she doesn't want to see me at all. I hate sixth grade! Life must get better!*

School ended. I didn't get together with Amy that summer—or ever again. Heather didn't include me in her clique, but she never kicked my ass, either. In fact, I don't remember much about what happened to them after we left Bayville Elementary School. When I started middle school the following September, I was the only student from my school in the honors classes and rarely crossed paths with anyone who had caused me so much misery.

I found friends among the brainiacs and creative kids, the true-blue kind I had so desperately hoped for. While I'd never again be the most popular girl in my grade, I did relearn how to take pride in being smart and funny.

And I still do.

# "That Kid"

## BY JANNI LEE SIMNER

Halfway through seventh grade, the girls from the lunch table reserved for the least popular kids came to me with a request: Could I please stop sitting with them? Their lives were hard enough already, they explained, and my being seen with them only made things worse.

I could say I was surprised, but I wasn't. Ever since kindergarten, I'd been *that* kid, after all. You know the one: the kid everyone picks on, the one it's okay, even expected, that you'll pick on, too. Even if you're one of the nice kids, the good kids, you don't dare to be friends with *that* kid, because it might look bad to your real friends, who you can't afford to lose.

For me, school had always been a day-in, day-out business of teasing and name-calling, of hair pulling and rock throwing. The teasing hurt more than the rocks. It began with accusations of cooties and babyishness, and progressed to taunts about my hair, my clothes, and my general unfitness to occupy space on this planet.

At least the adults in my life noticed, and even tried to do something about it. My elementary school lunch lady saw me sitting alone and invited me to help her clean dishes after lunch—a highly coveted job, partly because of the free ice cream that went with it. Helping in the kitchen kept me off the playground, where the rock throwing and name-calling were at their worst, and it made me feel a little bit important, like I mattered.

My elementary school principal let me read in the school office when there weren't enough dishes to keep me off the playground until class began. He also talked to the other kids, telling them that the way they were treating me wasn't right and that it had to stop. As far as I could tell, those talks didn't mean much to the others, but they meant something to me. They meant that someone else thought I didn't deserve this.

My mom also thought I didn't deserve this, and she told me, over and over again, what I probably most needed to hear: that school wasn't forever, and that things would get better one day. If she'd only said it once or twice, maybe I would have ignored her, but she said it so often that, eventually, I believed it. *Things would get better.* I had to hang on until they did.

It took a long time. The books I read helped a little, because in stories, things always got better, and downtrodden, abused, misunderstood, mistreated characters always triumphed in the end, one way or another.

In sixth grade, my mom transferred me to a different school, where I'd be with different kids. That should have helped, but by then I took every joke and insult personally, however slight. Within three days of starting at my new school, I was *that* kid once more. I lashed out and fought to the death when taunted. When one of my tormentors kicked me, I kicked her back, broke her finger, and got suspended. I stabbed a couple of kids with pencils, too, and got good at digging fingernails into skin.

Sixth grade was the worst year of my life. My teachers wondered why I cried all the time. All I really wanted, by then, was to be left alone.

My new school was bigger and less supportive than my old one. I don't remember anyone coming in to talk to the other kids. I do remember that by the end of the year there was a note in my file telling all my future teachers how dangerous I was.

Sixth grade should have been the year that broke me. Looking back, I don't understand why it didn't. But by seventh grade I'd begun writing, filling notebooks with stories of my own. Maybe that had something to do with it.

After all of that, being asked to leave the only lunch table that would have me seemed pretty minor. I wasn't even that upset, not really. Mostly it just felt awkward, and embarrassing, and—kind of a relief. I didn't have to pretend to be sort-of friends with those girls anymore—when we all knew better—just to have a place to sit. I was free.

Seventh grade was the year I stopped caring what other people thought. I would have friends who liked me and wanted me as I was, or I wouldn't have any friends at all. I sat alone, and it turned out sitting alone was better than pretending. People still teased me—I had a lot of cafeteria milk squirted in my face that year, and no one invited me to escape into the kitchen afterward—but by then squirted milk seemed pretty minor, too.

And after that—slowly, quietly—things did begin to get better. In eighth and ninth grades I made my first real friends, no pretending required.

But I have one more vivid bullying memory, from right before tenth grade, the year high school began in my town. That summer, a group of girls ganged up on me at the town pool, and as I kicked and pulled hair and dug in my fingernails and mostly just tried to get away, one of them said, "You think you're escaping. You think you're going to go to high school and that things will get better, but we *own* this town."

They were wrong. I did get away and things did keep getting better. High school wasn't perfect—people still whispered taunts in the halls—but compared to all the years before, it was pretty good. I had a circle of friends by then, and the teasing became background noise to my life instead of the thing that defined it.

Then in college, one day as I walked through the halls, I realized the whispers had gone away entirely, and that no one thought of me as *that* kid anymore.

I realized I'd made it through.

Yet this isn't over. Because no one deserves to be that kid. It isn't right, and it has to stop.

If you've ever shouted or whispered or posted a taunt online because everyone else was; if you've ever debated whether you dare talk to someone it isn't safe to be seen talking to; if you've ever wanted to tell your friends to back off but decided you'd better stay quiet—after all, your life is hard enough already—I want to say: you have a role to play in stopping it.

But if you are that kid, reading this now, what I want to say is this: It will get better. I promise you. I can't promise when. But I promise that it will.

# This Is Me

## BY ERIN DIONNE

This was me in seventh grade:

The tallest person in my class. Short hair, glasses, braces. Flute player in band. Newspaper reporter. Great student. Reader. Someone's best friend. Part of a group of girls who were smart and funny and into things like dance and science and horses and *Star Wars*. Sleepover attendee/thrower. Crushing on a boy. Swallowing hurt and shame and rage as the girls I'd been friends with in elementary school suddenly and mysteriously decided that my new friends weren't cool, my clothes weren't cool—I wasn't cool. Gritting my teeth as they snickered and whispered when I passed. Dodging venomous comments thrown my way in the hall. Player/ pawn in their mental games of Cold Shoulder, Catty Comment, Arched Eyebrow, and Flounce Away. Stressed out. Ulcers burning my stomach lining. Puking my guts up every morning before school. Puking after most meals. Swigging Mylanta out of the bottle. Scraping its minty-chalky outline off my lips. Missing weeks of classes to heal my burned and ulcerated stomach. Living on boiled chicken and mashed potatoes. Begging my mom not to get involved. Escaping into movies like *Pump Up the Volume*, *Heathers*, and *Revenge of the Nerds*. Confiding to my diary that I'd rather be anywhere, move anyplace, than have to deal.

In the middle of eighth grade: Dad's transfer to California.

Escape.

Relief.

This was me in college:

Average height, medium hair, contacts, great smile. Piccolo player in band. Writer. Great Student. Reader. Someone's girlfriend. Part of a group of people who are smart and funny and into things like dance and science and *Star Wars*. Dorm liver. Party attendee/thrower. Confident and funny. Walking into someone's apartment during a party. Spotting one of my junior high tormentors. Shaking. Trying to breathe. Stomach knotting. Hands clenching. Leaving because I couldn't deal with what came rushing up from the past. Spending the next year on edge at every school event. Keeping one eye out. Rehearsing what to say. Convincing myself not to be snarky. Fearing and wishing I'd see her.

Astonished and embarrassed by the power of nine-year-old words. Waiting, waiting, waiting. Running into her outside a classroom. Taking a deep breath. Listening. Mystified as she behaved like we were old friends. Struggling with the knowledge that I didn't matter to her while her behavior mattered so much to me. Coping with the fury that brought out. Understanding the yoke I'd lived under for so long. Casting it off.

This is me now:

Average height, medium hair, contacts, same smile. Teacher. Writer. Reader. Someone's wife. Someone's mom. Part of several groups of people who are smart and funny and into cool stuff like *Star Wars*. Home owner. Secure in myself. Proof of how much words hurt. Proof that word wounds and stomachs can heal. Using my story to help others.

# Bullies for Me

## BY MO WILLEMS

329

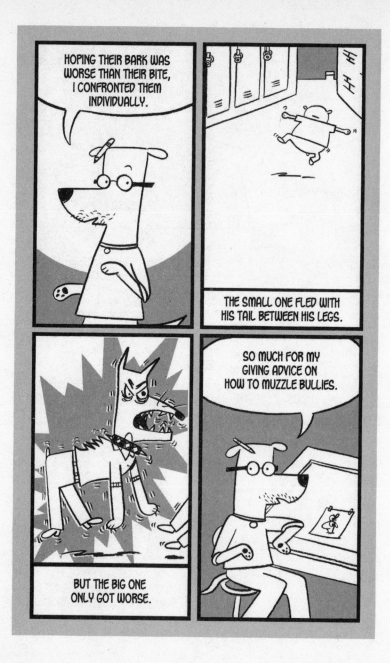

333

# To Carolyn Mackler,
## FROM ELIZABETH IN IL

Dear Ms. Mackler,

Hello, my name is Elizabeth and I am a sixth-grade girl. I really loved your book *The Earth, My Butt, and Other Big Round Things*. It is definitely one of my favorite books. The character Virginia Shreves really spoke to me in a way that no other character ever has. When I read this book, I felt like this was a book about me. I completely understand the way she felt in the bathroom when the Bri-girls were talking about her. I, having been ridiculed my whole life, would know that overhearing people trashing you is a lot worse than them saying it to your face. I feel like I couldn't be this happy without the inspiration your book gave me. I can feel every emotion she feels with all the description you gave. When she bites the insides of her cheeks, I can taste blood.

Whenever she cries, I can feel myself starting to tear up. I can especially feel the triumph of her rebellion. I think my favorite part is when she is in Seattle and she realizes she isn't numb anymore. Thank you for writing this amazing book. I have never loved a book the same way before. If possible, please send a response to my letter. I would really appreciate it. Thank you so much.

Yours truly,
Elizabeth

# Dear Elizabeth

## BY CAROLYN MACKLER

Dear Elizabeth,

I only just got your note. You must be in seventh grade by now! Every so often I receive a letter from a reader that makes me pause in my way-too-busy life (book deadlines and two young children), reflect on what I do, and feel moved by the fact that my novels might possibly speak to someone when they most need it. Thank you for writing that letter.

You said you've been ridiculed your whole life. While I wish I could wave a wand and evaporate all bullies and jerks (wouldn't that be great?), I can't. But I can say this: I totally sympathize. Before I get to my last paragraph—all about how someday you'll be in high school (slightly better) and college (even better) and then you'll hit the real world, where you can pick who you spend your days with (*not* people who ridicule you) and one day you'll have a way-too-busy life, surrounded by friends who love you for who you are . . . *before* I talk about all this, I want to acknowledge how hard it is to be in the trenches. Believe me, I was there.

It started when I was in seventh grade. Someone slipped a note in my locker. *Dear Carolyn*, the person had written. *Welcome to Hoser High.* I didn't know what a hoser was, but I had a sinking feeling that this couldn't be good. It went from bad to worse. Boys started teasing me about being Jewish. They coughed "Jew" behind their hand as I walked into the cafeteria. In French class, when we learned the word *jupe* (meaning *skirt*), it sounded enough like *Jew* to make them turn in their desks and snicker at me while I lowered my head, my cheeks burning, my insides dying. As the bullying continued—everything from a group of kids making fun of me for showing up at school with wet hair to boys wearing swastikas on Halloween—my self-esteem tanked. I started junior high happy and confident. Sure, I was a little quirky and I didn't care about clothes and I designed elaborate villages for my dolls, but at the beginning of sixth grade, I felt good about myself and my place in the world. By the end of eighth grade, I was skittish and nervous and insecure. I barely even liked myself anymore.

The hardest thing was that I didn't know where to turn. It helped to read novels about teenagers with different lives and hope that someday I would escape my conservative small town. I had my best friend, though she was a grade younger and didn't know how bad it was for me at school. I told my parents, who talked about it with the principal. But nothing got better. My teachers didn't even make the boys remove their swastikas on Halloween!

This was twenty-five years ago. Maybe things have changed in the schools. Hopefully they have. Hopefully, Elizabeth, you have an adult you can confide in, someone at school who can help you. I know it's tricky. I know that to tell someone risks calling further attention to yourself. I'm glad you were inspired by *The Earth, My Butt, and Other Big Round Things*. That was an important story for me to write, particularly when Virginia starts embracing herself as she is, not changing to please other people.

And this brings me to my inspiring last paragraph. The teasing subsided by the end of junior high. I went to high school and made new friends and had boyfriends and fell in love for the first time. I went to college and then became a novelist (my grown-up version of playing dolls!) and met my husband and got married and we now have two beautiful boys. No one teases me anymore. I feel safe in my life. Those hellish years are over.

Okay, one more paragraph. Because even though those years are over, they're not. Being bullied is part of who I am today—in the way I think, the way I treat people, the way I raise my children. It was scarring. Now and then I have to take a deep breath and fend off the inner voice that says I'm, well, a *hoser*. But it also made me a deeper, more sympathetic, more compassionate person. It's allowed me to write novels about teen characters and really feel what they are going through. Which, in turn, has resulted in letters from readers like you! Yes, I wish I'd never been bullied (enter magic wand here). But I'm writing to say that there's hope on the other side. Hang in there.

Love,
Carolyn

# Resources for Teens

**NATIONAL SUICIDE PREVENTION LIFELINE**
A twenty-four-hour, toll-free suicide prevention service available to anyone in suicidal crisis.
1-800-273-TALK (8255)
www.suicidepreventionlifeline.org

**THE BOYS TOWN NATIONAL HOTLINE**
A toll-free number available to kids, teens, and young adults at any time—if you're depressed, contemplating suicide, being physically or sexually abused, on the run, addicted, threatened by gang violence, fighting with a friend or parent, or if you are faced with an overwhelming challenge.
1-800-448-3000
www.boystown.org/national-hotline
www.yourlifeyourvoice.org

**NATIONAL SEXUAL ASSAULT HOTLINE AND NATIONAL SEXUAL ASSAULT *ONLINE* HOTLINE**

A free, confidential, secure service that provides live help operated by RAINN via their telephone hotline or website.
1-800-656-HOPE
www.rainn.org/get-help

**TREVOR PROJECT**

The Trevor Project is determined to end suicide among LGBTQ youth by providing life-saving and life-affirming resources including their nationwide, twenty-four/seven crisis intervention lifeline, digital community, and advocacy/educational programs that create a safe, supportive, and positive environment for everyone.
www.thetrevorproject.org

**REACH OUT**

Reach Out is an information and support service that uses evidence-based principles and technology to help teens facing tough times and struggling with mental health issues. All content is written by teens, for teens.
http://us.reachout.com

**THE JED FOUNDATION**

The Jed Foundation works nationally to reduce the rate of suicide and the prevalence of emotional distress among

college and university students.
www.jedfoundation.org

**IT GETS BETTER PROJECT**
The suicide of fifteen-year-old Billy Lucas inspired "Savage Love" columnist Dan Savage's website, where musicians, politicians, artists, and many, many more talk openly about growing up gay—and sharing how life got better.
www.itgetsbetter.org

**RAVEN DAYS**
"For surviving middle school, junior high school, and high school as a hunted outsider." An organization for outsiders who are being bullied at school, for adults who remember what it was like to be bullied, and for those who want to help.
www.ravendays.org

# Resources for Educators and Parents

**STOMP OUT BULLYING**

Stomp Out Bullying, a national antibullying and anti-cyberbullying program for kids and teens, is a program of Love Our Children USA.

www.stompoutbullying.org

**TEACHING TOLERANCE**

Teaching Tolerance, a program of the Southern Poverty Law Center, aims to reduce prejudice and improve intergroup relations in the nation's classrooms and communities. Teaching Tolerance's Mix It Up program is a national campaign that helps K–12 teachers develop inclusive school communities.

www.tolerance.org

**INTERNATIONAL BULLYING PREVENTION ASSOCIATION**
The mission of the International Bullying Prevention Association is to support and enhance quality research-based bullying prevention principles and practices in order to achieve safe school climates, healthy work environments, good citizenship, and civic responsibility.
www.stopbullyingworld.org

**GLSEN**
The Gay, Lesbian, and Straight Education Network, the leading national education organization focused on ensuring safe schools for all students, envisions a world in which every child learns to respect and accept all people, regardless of sexual orientation or gender identity/expression.
www.glsen.org

**MASSACHUSETTS AGGRESSION REDUCTION CENTER**
The MARC website offers free resources on bullying prevention, cyberbullying education and prevention, and violence prevention.
www.bridgew.edu/marc

**STOP BULLYING NOW!**
A campaign that presents practical, research-based strategies to reduce bullying in schools.
www.stopbullyingnow.com

## NATIONAL ORGANIZATION FOR PEOPLE OF COLOR AGAINST SUICIDE

NOPCAS was formed to stop the tragic epidemic of suicide in minority communities.

www.nopcas.com

## THE OPHELIA PROJECT

The Ophelia Project serves youth and adults who are affected by relational and other nonphysical forms of aggression by providing them with a unique combination of tools, strategies, and solutions.

www.opheliaproject.org

# Acknowledgments

Thanks to all of the brilliant, generous, and talented contributors in this book. When we started the Young Adult Authors Against Bullying group on Facebook, we had no idea how quickly it would take off. So, not only do I want to thank the anthology contributors for their time, patience, and creativity, I'd like to thank the hundreds of authors who submitted essays for inclusion in this book (and who will be featured at www.dearbully.com), as well as the thousands who joined our fight against bullying online.

A huge thanks to HarperTeen's editors, Sarah Dotts Barley and Tara Weikum, for their guidance and wisdom. Thank you to our agents Elisabeth Weed and Edward Necarsulmer. I'd personally like to thank Jocelyn and Gloria Kelley of Kelley & Hall Book Publicity for immediately jumping behind this project and helping to promote it so that we received great media coverage, including Sheila Weller's amazing feature article in *Glamour* magazine.

And finally, I want to remember the teens that were the inspiration for this book and who tragically took their own lives because they couldn't see the light at the end of the tunnel: Phoebe Prince, Carl Walker-Hoover, Ty Field, and Tyler Clementi—to name only a few. This book is in your honor.

Bullying is not a rite of passage, it is not acceptable, and by working together, we can make it stop.

—Megan Kelley Hall

This book would not exist without two things: stories and bravery. Writers lived through the stories of this book. Stories of others' suffering now inspired us and them into action. For many of the contributors here and on the website, it took immense bravery to share those stories. Thank you all so much.

A special thanks to the contributors, all authors of awesome. Thanks to Sarah Dotts Barley, Tara Weikum, Caroline Sun, and the entire Harper team for making this book a reality. It was a giant leap of faith and a huge squat press of hard work on their parts. Similar thanks goes to Edward Necarsulmer IV and Elisabeth Weed, both mighty vanquishers of meanness. I will be forever grateful for the passion and integrity you all brought to this project.

Thanks also to everyone who has ever survived. That includes the bullied, the bullies, the bystanders, and the heroes. We have a little bit of all of these in each of us. This book is for you.

And finally, thank you to Emily Ciciotte and Shaun Farrar, who taught me how to be tough.

—Carrie Jones

# Contributors

CYN BALOG is the author of the paranormal novels *Fairy Tale*, *Sleepless*, and *Starstruck*. She lives outside Allentown, Pennsylvania, with her husband and daughters. Visit her online at www.cynbalog.com.

LISE BERNIER is a retired molecular biologist with a specialty in genetics. She has always been an artist on the side. "They Made Me Do It and I'm Sorry" is her first comic. She lives in Montreal, Canada, and is Cecil Castellucci's mother.

HEATHER BREWER is the author of the *New York Times* bestselling series The Chronicles of Vladimir Tod; *First Kill*, the first book in The Slayer Chronicles; and *Bloodbound*, a romantic fantasy epic. Heather likes moonlit walks, black nail polish, and the feeling of sand between her toes. She lives in Saint Louis, Missouri, with her husband, two children, and two very spoiled cats. Visit her online at www.heatherbrewer.com.

JESSICA BRODY is the author of *The Karma Club*, *My Life Undecided*, *52 Reasons to Hate My Father*, *Unremembered*, and two books for adults. Jessica originally moved to Los Angeles to be a singer/songwriter, but soon discovered she had a better knack for writing novels. Now she uses her songwriting background to write and produce original soundtracks for her books. Visit her online at www.jessicabrody.com.

TERI BROWN really did grow up in Alfalfa. She now lives in Portland, Oregon, with her husband and two teenagers. She is the author of *Read My Lips*. Visit her online at www.teribrownwrites.com.

CECIL CASTELLUCCI is the author of numerous books for young adults, including *Rose Sees Red, Beige, The Queen of Cool, Boy Proof*, and The Plain Janes graphic novel series. She lives in Los Angeles. Visit her online at www.misscecil.com.

CRISSA-JEAN CHAPPELL teaches creative writing and cinema studies at Miami International University of Art and Design. She is the author of *Total Constant Order*, which was a New York Public Library Book for the Teen Age, a Florida Book Award medalist, and a *VOYA* Editor's Choice, and *NARC*. She no longer wishes for superpowers of invisibility, though sometimes she flies in her dreams. Visit her online at www.crissajeanchappell.com.

MARINA COHEN is the author of several works of fiction and nonfiction, including three middle grade novels, *Shadow of the Moon, Trick of the Light*, and *Chasing the White Witch*, and two teen thrillers, *Ghost Ride* and *Mind Gap*. *Ghost Ride* was shortlisted by the Ontario Library Association for their Red Maple Award. Marina lives in Markham, Ontario, Canada, with her husband and three children.

HOLLY CUPALA is the author of *Tell Me a Secret* and *Don't Breathe a Word*, which was inspired by her real-life abusive relationships chronicled in "Midsummer's Nightmare." When she isn't writing her next novel or making art, Holly spends time with her family in Seattle, Washington. A portion of her author earnings goes to World Vision's Hope for Sexually Exploited Girls. You can find Holly online at www.hollycupala.com.

ERIN DIONNE survived junior high bullying and is now the author of *Models Don't Eat Chocolate Cookies, The Total Tragedy of a Girl Named Hamlet*, and

*Notes from an Accidental Band Geek.* Her novels are about fitting in, figuring things out, and finding yourself. She lives outside of Boston with her family and dog, where she roots for the Red Sox, teaches English at an art college, and enjoys chocolate cookies. Visit her online at www.erindionne.com.

**LUCIENNE DIVER** is the author of the Vamped series, which *VOYA* calls "witty vampire romance/adventure with plenty of heart and action" and Wondrous Reads calls "*Mean Girls* with fangs." Either description will do. Lucienne is also a longtime book addict, a literary agent, a blogger, a mom, and a caffeine enthusiast. More information is available online at www.luciennediver.com.

**CLAUDIA GABEL** is the author of the teen series In or Out and the mash-up novel *Romeo & Juliet & Vampires.* She is also a senior editor at Katherine Tegen Books, an imprint of HarperCollins Children's Books, where she acquires and develops fiction for young readers. She lives in New York City. You can visit her online at www.claudiagabel.com and check out her blog at www.claudiagabel.blogspot.com.

**NANCY GARDEN** is a recipient of the American Library Association's Margaret A. Edwards Award for lifetime achievement in writing books for teens. She is the author of the classic *Annie on My Mind*, one of the first teen novels to feature lesbian characters positively, among many other books. Visit her online at www.nancygarden.com.

**JEANNINE GARSEE** works as a psychiatric nurse in a busy inner-city hospital and lives with her family outside Cleveland. She is the author of *Say the Word*; *Before, After, and Somebody in Between*; and *The Unquiet*. Visit her online at www.jeanninegarsee.com.

**LINDA GERBER** is the author of *Trance,* the Death By . . . mystery series, *Now and Zen, The Finnish Line,* and *Celebrity.* Her books have been tapped as ALA Popular Paperbacks for Young Adults and Junior Library Guild and Literacy Lab Selections. Linda recently returned to life in the Midwest after four years in Japan, where she served as the Regional Advisor for the Tokyo chapter of the Society of Children's Book Writers and Illustrators. She lives and writes in

Dublin, Ohio, blissfully ignoring her husband, four kids, and one very naughty puppy. Visit her online at www.lindagerber.com.

MEGAN KELLEY HALL, in addition to coediting this book, is the author of *Sisters of Misery* and *The Lost Sister*, two teen gothic thrillers that tackled bullying and "mean girls" way before bullying became daily news. Megan is a founding partner with her mother and sister of Kelley & Hall Book Publicity and has written for a variety of publications, including *Elle*, *Glamour*, *Parenting*, *American Baby*, *Working Mother*, the *Boston Globe*, and the *Boston Herald*. A graduate of Skidmore College, she lives north of Boston with her husband and her daughter. Visit her online at www.megankelleyhall.com.

KRISTIN HARMEL, a longtime reporter for *People*, is the author of *The Art of French Kissing*, *Italian for Beginners*, *The Blonde Theory*, *How to Sleep with a Movie Star*, and the teen novel *After*. She has lived in Paris, Los Angeles, New York, Boston, and Miami, and now resides primarily in Orlando. Visit her online at www.kristinharmel.com.

When NANCY HOLDER was sixteen, she dropped out of high school to become a ballet dancer in Cologne, Germany. Eventually she returned home to California and graduated from the University of California, San Diego. A four-time winner of the Bram Stoker Award from the Horror Writers Association, Nancy has received accolades from the American Library Association, the American Reading Association, the New York Public Library, and *Romantic Times*. She and Debbie Viguié coauthored the *New York Times* bestselling series Wicked, *Crusade*, and the Wolf Springs Chronicles. Nancy is also the author of the teen horror series Possessions and has written many novels set in the *Buffy the Vampire Slayer*, *Angel*, *Saving Grace*, *Hellboy*, and *Smallville* universes. Visit her online at www.nancyholder.com.

ELLEN HOPKINS is the *New York Times* bestselling author of *Crank*, *Burned*, *Impulse*, *Glass*, *Identical*, and *Perfect*. Visit her online at www.ellenhopkins.com.

TONYA HURLEY is the author of the instant *New York Times* bestselling and critically acclaimed ghostgirl series, and *Blessed*, the beginning of a new trilogy. A writer for television and film as well, Tonya has created, produced, and written live and animated series for ABC, and her independent films have been selected for such prestigious film festivals as Tribeca, Edinburgh, and the LA Independent, and broadcast on IFC, the Sundance Channel, and PBS. Tonya lives in New York with her husband and daughter. Visit her online at www.tonyahurley.com.

CARRIE JONES (the writer, not the porn star, and this book's coeditor) has been battling bullies ever since they told her she talked funny. She's pretty sure she still talks funny, but it hasn't kept her from being an internationally bestselling author of the Need series or winning awards for some of her other books. It also hasn't kept her from being an undercover prostitute, a church secretary, a police dispatcher, or a gymnastics instructor. Carrie is also the author of *After Obsession*, cowritten with Steven E. Wedel. She lives in Maine with two ridiculously large dogs and the rest of her family. None of them mind how she talks either. Visit her online at www.carriejonesbooks.com.

*New York Times* bestselling author SOPHIE JORDAN grew up in the Texas hill country, where she wove fantasies of dragons, warriors, and princesses. Sophie is a former high school English teacher and her debut young adult novel, *Firelight*, is out now. Visit her online at www.sophiejordan.net.

LAURA KASISCHKE has published several novels, including *The Raising* and two novels for teens, *Boy Heaven* and *Feathered*, and eight collections of poetry. She is a professor in the MFA program and at the Residential College at the University of Michigan. She lives with her husband and son in Chelsea, Michigan.

LAUREN KATE grew up in Dallas, went to school in Atlanta, and started writing in New York. She is the *New York Times* bestselling author of the Fallen series and *The Betrayal of Natalie Hargrove*. She lives in Laurel Canyon, California, with her husband and hopes to work in a restaurant kitchen, get a dog, and learn how to surf. Visit her online at www.laurenkatebooks.net.

JOCELYN MAEVE KELLEY is a literary publicist and freelance journalist, writing for national magazines like *Glamour, Self, Elle,* and *The Writer*. A magna cum laude graduate of Emerson College, Jocelyn hosted and produced an award-winning Associated Press public affairs radio program that tackled subjects such as bullying, depression, and school systems in America. Visit her online at www.kelleyandhall.com.

**DEBORAH KERBEL** is the author of *Lure, Girl on the Other Side,* and *Mackenzie, Lost and Found. Girl on the Other Side,* which deals with the subject of bullying in school, was shortlisted by the Canadian Library Association for its Young Adult Book Award. Born in London, Deborah currently lives and writes in Thornhill, Ontario, with her husband and two children. Visit her online at www.deborahkerbel.com.

**A. S. KING** is the author of the ALA Best Book for Young Adults *The Dust of 100 Dogs*; the Michael L. Printz Honor Book *Please Ignore Vera Dietz*, described as "deeply suspenseful and profoundly human" by *Publishers Weekly*, and *Everybody Sees the Ants*. Recently returned from Ireland, where she spent more than a decade living off the land, breeding rare poultry, teaching literacy, and writing novels, she now lives deep in the Pennsylvania woods with her husband and children. Learn more online at www.as-king.com.

**JO KNOWLES**, author of *Lessons from a Dead Girl, Jumping Off Swings*, and *Pearl*, lives in Vermont with her husband and son. Visit her online at www.joknowles.com or follow her blog at www.jbknowles.livejournal.com.

**AMY GOLDMAN KOSS** is the author of several novels, including *The Not-So-Great Depression, Poison Ivy*, and *Side Effects*. She lives in California with her husband and children. Visit her online at www.amygoldmankoss.net.

**STEPHANIE KUEHNERT** was born in St. Louis, Missouri, in 1979. She got her start like most authors by writing bad poetry about unrequited love and razor blades back in the eighth grade, also around the time she discovered punk rock. Stephanie is the author of *I Wanna Be Your Joey Ramone* and *Ballads of Suburbia*. Visit her online at www.stephaniekuehnert.com.

Although ERIC LUPER took his fair share of being force-fed grass on the soccer field and being pushed into his locker after gym class, he found himself on the other side of it all a stronger, more compassionate human being. Now he is the author of numerous books for young people, including *Jeremy Bender vs. the Cupcake Cadets* and *Seth Baumgartner's Love Manifesto*. (By the way, guess how many of those bullies have written books? None!) To learn more, visit Eric online at www.ericluper.com.

CAROLYN MACKLER is the author of the Michael L. Printz Honor Book *The Earth, My Butt, and Other Big Round Things, Tangled, Guyaholic, Vegan Virgin Valentine*, and *Love and Other Four-Letter Words*. Carolyn lives in New York City with her husband and two young sons. Visit her online at www.carolynmackler.com.

MEGAN McCAFFERTY is the author of *Bumped*. She also wrote the *New York Times* bestselling Jessica Darling series, which includes the novels *Sloppy Firsts, Second Helpings, Charmed Thirds, Fourth Comings*, and *Perfect Fifths*. She lives in New Jersey with her husband and son. For more information, follow @meganmccafferty on Twitter, friend her on Facebook, or visit her online at www.meganmccafferty.com.

LISA McMANN is the *New York Times* bestselling author of the Wake trilogy, *Cryer's Cross*, and *Dead to You*, and the dystopian fantasy series The Unwanteds for younger readers. Before writing novels, Lisa worked as a blueberry picker, a bindery worker in a printing company, an independent bookseller, and a realtor. Lisa grew up in Michigan and lived there until 2004. Now she lives in the Phoenix area with her husband and two teenagers. Read more about Lisa at www.lisamcmann.com or find her on Facebook (www.facebook.com/McMannFan) or Twitter (@lisa_mcmann).

DAWN METCALF, the author of *Luminous*, has no good excuse for the way she writes. She lived in a normal, loving, suburban home, studied hard, went to college, went to graduate school, got married, had babies, and settled down in northern Connecticut. Despite this wholesome lifestyle, she has been clearly corrupted by fairy tales, puppet visionaries, British humor, and graphic novels. As a result, she writes dark, quirky, and sometimes humorous speculative fiction. Visit her online at www.dawnmetcalf.com.

SAUNDRA MITCHELL has been a phone psychic, a car salesperson, a denture delivery person, and a layout waxer. She's dodged trains, endured basic training, and hitchhiked from Montana to California. She teaches herself languages, raises children, and makes paper for fun. She's also a screenwriter for Fresh Films and the author of *Shadowed Summer*, *The Vespertine*, and *The Springsweet*. She always picks truth; dares are too easy. Visit her online at www.saundramitchell.com.

R. A. NELSON is the author of the novels *Teach Me*, *Breathe My Name*, *Days of Little Texas*, and *Throat*. He was chosen as a *Horn Book* Newcomer, and his books have been recognized by the Parents' Choice Awards, the New York Public Library Books for the Teen Age list, and Book Sense Kid Picks, and have been nominated to the YALSA Best Books for Young Adults list. Nelson lives with his family in northern Alabama and works at NASA's Marshall Space Flight Center. Visit him online at www.ranelsonbooks.com.

ALYSON NOËL is the number one *New York Times* bestselling author of the Immortals series (*Evermore*, *Blue Moon*, *Shadowland*, *Dark Flame*, *Night Star*, and the sixth and final book, *Everlasting*); the Immortals spin-off series beginning with *Radiance*; *Faking 19*; and *Art Geeks and Prom Queens*. She lives in Laguna Beach, California. Visit her online at www.alysonnoel.com.

LAUREN OLIVER comes from a family of writers and has always been an avid reader. She graduated from the University of Chicago, attended the MFA program at New York University, and worked briefly as the world's worst editorial assistant, and only marginally better assistant editor, at a major publishing house in New York. Her major career contributions during this time were flouting the corporate dress code and breaking the printer. Her debut novel, *Before I Fall*, was a *New York Times* bestseller. She is also the author of *Delirium* and her debut novel for younger readers, *Liesl & Po*. Visit her online at www.laurenoliverbooks.com.

MICOL OSTOW is half Puerto Rican, half Jewish, half reader, half writer, and, when under deadline, often half asleep. Micol was working as an editor of young adult fiction when she began to write her own books; since then, she has published more than 40 works for readers of all ages. She is the author of *Emily Goldberg Learns to Salsa*, a New York Public Library Book for the Teen Age, the graphic novel hybrid *So Punk Rock (And Other Ways to Disappoint Your Mother)*, a Sydney Taylor Notable Book for Teens, and the novel in verse *family*, loosely based on the Manson family murders of 1969. Visit her online at www.micolostow.com.

MARLENE PEREZ is the author of the Dead Is series, *The Comeback*, and *Love in the Corner Pocket*. She lives in Orange County, California. Visit her online at www.marleneperez.com.

APRILYNNE PIKE is the number one *New York Times* bestselling author of the Wings series, which includes *Wings*, *Spells*, and *Illusions*. She lives in Arizona with her husband and three kids. Visit her online at www.aprillynnepike.com.

AMY REED was born and raised around Seattle, where she attended a total of eight schools by the time she was eighteen. After a brief stint at Reed College (no relation), she moved to San Francisco and spent the next several years serving coffee and getting into trouble. She eventually graduated from film school and is now the author of *Beautiful* and *Clean*. Visit her online at www.amyreedfiction.com.

DEBBIE RIGAUD began her writing career covering news and entertainment for magazines, including *Seventeen, Twist,* and *CosmoGIRL!*. She's interviewed celebs, politicians, and other social figures, but enjoyed interviewing "real girls" the most. A total Jersey girl at heart, Debbie lives in Bermuda with her husband. Catch her on bookshelves (*Perfect Shot* and *Hallway Diaries*) and online at www.debbierigaud.com.

CARRIE RYAN is the *New York Times* bestselling author of several critically acclaimed novels set decades after the zombie apocalypse: *The Forest of Hands and Teeth*, which was named to the ALA Best Books for Young Adults, Chicago Public Library Best of the Best, and New York Public Library Stuff for the Teen

Age lists; *The Dead-Tossed Waves*; and *The Dark and Hollow Places*. Her books have been translated into more than a dozen languages. Carrie is a graduate of Williams College and Duke University School of Law. A former litigator, she now writes full time and lives with her husband (who is even more amazing than a cowboy) in Charlotte, North Carolina. Visit her online at www.carrieryan.com.

**KURTIS SCALETTA** was born in Louisiana and grew up in New Mexico, North Dakota, England, Liberia, Brazil, and a few other places. His books for young readers include *Mudville*, which was an ALA *Booklist* "Top 10 Sports Books for Youth"; *Mamba Point*, which *Kirkus Reviews*, in a starred review, called an "expertly voiced narrative . . . tinted with magical realism that is by turns scary and very funny"; and *The Tanglewood Terror*. Kurtis now lives in Minneapolis with his wife, their son, and several cats. To learn more about him and his books, visit him online at www.kurtisscaletta.com.

**MELISSA SCHORR** is the author of *Goy Crazy*, a romantic comedy about interfaith dating that was named a New York Public Library Book for the Teen Age. A graduate of the Bronx High School of Science and Northwestern University, Melissa was a Knight Science Journalism Fellow at MIT. She currently works and lives as a journalist outside Boston with her two daughters, her husband, and their terrier, Bailey. Visit her online at www.melissaschorr.com.

**LISA SCHROEDER** is a native Oregonian and lives there still with her husband and two sons. She is the author of three novels in verse for young adults: *I Heart You, You Haunt Me*; *Far from You*; and *Chasing Brooklyn*. Visit her online at www.lisaschroederbooks.com.

**JON SCIESZKA** was born in Flint, Michigan, on September 8, 1954. He grew up with five brothers, has the same birthday as Peter Sellers and the Virgin Mary, and has a sneaking suspicion that the characters in his Dick and Jane reader were not of this world. Those plain facts, plus his elementary school principal dad, Louis; his registered nurse mom, Shirley; *Mad* magazine; four years of premed undergrad; *The Rocky and Bullwinkle Show*; an MFA in fiction from Columbia University; Robert Benchley; five years of painting apartments in New York City; his lovely wife, Jeri Hansen, who introduced him to Molly Leach and Lane Smith; *Green Eggs and Ham*; his teenage daughter, Casey, and almost teenage son, Jake; ten years of teaching a little bit of everything from first grade to eighth grade; and the last twenty years of living in Brooklyn . . . are just some of Jon's answers to the questions "Where do you get your ideas?" and/or "How did you become a writer?" Visit him online at www.jsworldwide.com.

KIERAN SCOTT is the author of the She's So Dead to Us trilogy, the Non-Blonde Cheerleader trilogy, and *Geek Magnet*. In her spare time, Kieran writes the *New York Times* bestselling Private and Privilege series under the pseudonym Kate Brian, and has written several other novels under that name. Kieran has lived in New Jersey all her life (but looks nothing like Snooki), and graduated from Rutgers University with honors. Kieran loves to bake, read YA, watch football (Go Giants!), take Pilates classes, and ride her bike with her husband and son. Also, she's kind of obsessed with TV. You can find out more online at www.kieranscott.net, or follow her on Twitter @kieranscott.

COURTNEY SHEINMEL, author of *My So-Called Family*, *Positively*, and *Sincerely*, grew up in California and New York. She is a graduate of Barnard College of Columbia University and Fordham University School of Law. Visit her online at www.courtneysheinmel.com.

MELODYE SHORE vowed in third grade that she would grow up to be the kind of teacher she wished she'd had. For much of her professional life, she did just that. As a teacher of English, reading, and other subjects, she worked primarily with underprepared and disadvantaged students. And as president of the National Association of Developmental Education (NADE), she helped make them visible to a broader audience across the United States and in other countries. Her current book project chronicles an itinerant childhood, in which Melodye and her family crisscrossed the country in a cramped sedan, holding revival meetings wherever they landed. While she still enjoys traveling, Melodye feels most at home in Southern California, where she lives with her husband. Visit her online at www.melodyeshore.com.

JANNI LEE SIMNER has published three books for teens: *Bones of Faerie*, its sequel, *Faerie Winter*, and *Thief Eyes*. She is also the author of four books for younger readers and more than 30 short stories. Visit her online at www.simner.com.

CYNTHIA LEITICH SMITH is the *New York Times* bestselling author of the gothic fantasies *Tantalize, Eternal,* and *Blessed.* She also has written several short stories for teens as well as award-winning books for younger readers. She is a tribally enrolled citizen of the Muscogee (Creek) Nation and makes her home in Austin, Texas, with her husband and sometimes coauthor Greg Leitich Smith. She is also on the faculty of the Vermont College of Fine Arts Writing for Children and Young Adults MFA program. Visit her online at www.cynthialeitichsmith.com.

So far, R.L. STINE's books, including the Fear Street and Goosebumps series, have sold over 300 million copies. He lives in New York City. Visit him online at www.rlstine.com.

LAURIE FARIA STOLARZ is the author of *Deadly Little Secret, Deadly Little Lies, Deadly Little Games, Deadly Little Voices, Project 17,* and *Bleed,* as well as the bestselling Blue Is for Nightmares series. Born and raised in Salem, Massachusetts, Laurie attended Merrimack College and received an MFA in creative writing from Emerson College in Boston. For more information, visit her online at www.lauriestolarz.com.

Award-winning author TANYA LEE STONE writes for kids and teens. Her books include the teen novel *A Bad Boy Can Be Good for a Girl* and nonfiction for older readers *The Good, The Bad, and the Barbie: A Doll's History and Her Impact on Us* and *Almost Astronauts: 13 Women Who Dared to Dream.* Her work has received the Robert F. Sibert Medal, a *Boston Globe–Horn Book* Award Honor, and the Bank Street College of Education's Flora Steiglitz Straus Award. She teaches writing at Champlain College. Visit her online at www.tanyastone.com.

RACHEL VAIL is a multiple award-winning author of more than thirty books for children and teenagers. Her novels include *Justin Case: School, Drool, and Other Daily Disasters*; the Avery Sisters Trilogy (*Lucky, Gorgeous,* and *Brilliant*); *If We Kiss;* and the Friendship Ring series. Rachel lives in New York City with her husband and two sons. You can visit her online at www.rachelvail.com.

MELISSA WALKER is a writer who has worked as the *ELLEgirl* features editor and *Seventeen* prom editor. All in the name of journalism, she has spent twenty-four hours with male models and attended an elite finishing school for girls in New Zealand, among other hardships. Melissa is the author of *Lovestruck Summer*, *Violet on the Runway*, *Violet by Design*, and *Violet in Private*. She graduated from Vassar College and lives in Brooklyn. Visit her online at www.melissacwalker.com.

Born to a Puerto Rican father and a Polish mother, DIANA RODRIGUEZ WALLACH has experienced the cultures that her characters live in. Her debut novel was *Amor and Summer Secrets*. She has worked as a reporter and as an advocate for inner-city public schools. She currently lives in Philadelphia with her husband. Visit her online at www.dianarodriguezwallach.com.

DANIEL WATERS is the author of the Generation Dead series. Visit him online at www.watersdan.blogspot.com.

SARA BENNETT WEALER grew up in Kansas and now lives in Ohio with her husband and daughters. She is the author of *Rival*. Visit her online at www.sarabennettwealer.com.

STEVEN E. WEDEL is a lifelong Oklahoman. He's held many jobs, including machinist and journalist, but is currently a high school English teacher. He is the coauthor, with Carrie Jones, of *After Obsession*. Visit Steven online at www.stevenewedel.com.

NANCY WERLIN is the author of eight YA novels so far, which include *The Killer's Cousin* (winner of the Edgar Award), *The Rules of Survival* (a National Book Award finalist), *Impossible* (a *New York Times* bestseller), and *Extraordinary* (an Amazon.com Top 10 Book). She lives near Boston with her husband, Jim McCoy. Visit her online at www.nancywerlin.com.

KIERSTEN WHITE is the *New York Times* bestselling author of *Paranormalcy* and its sequel, *Supernaturally*. She has one tall husband and two small children and lives near the ocean in San Diego. Visit her online at www.kierstenwhite.com.

Three-time Caldecott honoree MO WILLEMS is known for his bestselling picture books featuring Pigeons, Knuffle Bunnies, and Elephant & Piggies. Work for older audiences includes the cartoon travelog *You Can Never Find a Rickshaw When It Monsoons* and works in *Every Man for Himself*, *Guys Read*, and the Monkeysuit comix anthologies. Mo created the Cartoon Network's *Sheep in the Big City* and was the head writer for *Codename: Kids Next Door* before making books. Visit him online at www.mowillems.com.

MARYROSE WOOD, a former Broadway actor, comedian, and playwright, is proud to be a contributor to this anthology. She is the author of *The Mysterious Howling* and *The Hidden Gallery*, the first two volumes of The Incorrigible Children of Ashton Place series, The Poison Diaries, a gothic trilogy for teens based on a concept by the Duchess of Northumberland, *My Life: The Musical*, and *Why I Let My Hair Grow Out*. For more information, visit her online at www.maryrosewood.com.

LISA YEE is the author of ten novels, including *Millicent Min, Girl Genius*, recipient of the Sid Fleischman Humor Award; her Bobby Ellis-Chan series for younger readers; *Absolutely Maybe*, for teens; and *Warp Speed*, which follows seventh grader Marley Sandlesky, a *Star Trek* geek who gets beat up every day at school. A Thurber House Children's Writer-in-Residence, Lisa has been named a *Publishers Weekly* Flying Start and a *USA Today* Critics' Top Pick. Lisa lives in South Pasadena, California, with her family. You can visit her online at www.lisayee.com or check out her blog at www.lisayee.livejournal.com.

LARA ZEISES is the author of six books for teenagers, including *Contents Under Pressure* and *The Sweet Life of Stella Madison*. Her novel *True Confessions of a Hollywood Starlet* (published under the pseudonym Lola Douglas) was made into a Lifetime movie. Lara earned her MFA in creative writing from Emerson College. She works for the International Reading Association and leads fiction workshops at the University of Delaware. You can visit her online at www.zeisgeist.com.

MICHELLE ZINK has always been fascinated with ancient myths and legends. Never satisfied with simply reading them, she usually ends up asking,

"What if?" Sometimes asking only leads to more questions, but every now and then, when everything falls into place just right, a story is born. *Prophecy of the Sisters*, *Guardian of the Gate*, and *Circle of Fire* were three of those stories. She lives in New York. Visit her online at www.michellezink.com.

# Copyright (continued)